Your Life *Is Your*

Masterpiece

Practical Tips to Design
Your Own Life with Purpose

Dr. Cesar Vargas

Doctor of Clinical Hypnotherapy

CESAR VARGAS, PH.D.

Editing & Formatting: Dr. Cesar Vargas

Cover Design: Katrin Shumakov

Visit YourLifeIsYourMasterpiece.com to learn about our live trainings on Creating Your Life as Your Masterpiece, Certain Goals Workshop, Hypnosis, Neuro-Linguistic Programming, and more!

Veritas Invictus Publishing
8502 East Chapman Avenue # 302
Orange, California 92869

ISBN 978-1-939180-01-8

www.*Your*Life*Is Your Masterpiece*.com

DEDICATION

This book is dedicated to each and every one of my students, clients and seminar participants, all of whom have taught me something about the best application of these principles in the most practical of situations.

To all my teachers and mentors, for sharing liberally and completely, and trusting me with this powerful knowledge... what have you done?!?

Finally, to Ali. Because Life Is Awesome, when You Create It!
Learn it, Live it, Love it! I'm Proud of You!

CONTENTS

✦ ✦ ✦

$\mathcal{I}$NTRODUCTION

✦ ✦ ✦

SOME TIME AGO, I WAS LISTENING to Joe Vitale's Clearing Audio program, part of which are some affirmations set to trance-inducing music, which help you shape a new way of thinking and clear away disempowering beliefs about yourself, your life, and the way you see things in general.

I have followed Joe's work, from *The Power of Outrageous Marketing*, to all of the *Hypnotic Writing* series to his latest (at the time of this writing) *The Awakening Course*. I love the way he gives freely from his own experience; so much so that I offered to translate into Spanish his *Spiritual Marketing* book, which then evolved into *The Attractor Factor*.

As I was listening to this Clearing Audio, one particular phrase resonated with me... it seemed as though this phrase just jumped straight out of the CD player and into the very core of my being. The phrase was "You are the Michelangelo of your own life; the David you're sculpting is you."

It's profound, isn't it? Think about it!

1

EVERYTHING we do (or don't do) in our lives, every moment of every day, with every decision we make, we are creating... no... we are SCULPTING our own life.

As a successful Master Practitioner and Trainer of Neuro-Linguistic Programming, people often come to me and say, "I realize I can create my own reality and be in control of my own mind, but HOW do I do it?"

The answer is in this book.

When you realize that YOU and only you have control of your life, the next question is obvious: HOW?

Do you have a couple of hours to invest so you can design the life of your dreams? I'm absolutely positive that, no matter who you are or where you are, I can teach you how you can have exactly what you want, exactly the way you want it – or something even better than you thought possible.

How can I be so certain that this can be done?

It's simple. It's a matter of learning about your mind, how it works, and using a simple method to make that amazing machine do everything you want it to do to give you a life that you love, a life that you yourself define.

You might wonder how anyone can know for sure that it can work for him or her. To put it simply, if you can read these words, the process will work for you, because we all have a brain; and that's what we're going to talk about and help you communicate with. Even if we don't know each other personally, this I can tell you: We all have a mind, and if we knew that it's just like a computer ready for you to program your life into it using your own design talents, you'd understand that you are the programmer of your life. Maybe you ought to get some training so that the computer does exactly and predictably what you want it to do. Being that we agree now that *Your Life Is Your Masterpiece*, in order to get you the best art training, and the largest painter pallet and the widest variety of brushes you can have, so that you CREATE YOUR MASTERPIECE in marvelous and amazing ways, you must learn the techniques.

We are all unique human beings, carrying our own hopes and dreams. Along with them are your own fears and self-driven limitations. They trap your own magnificent potential, not allowing it to surface and contribute your beauty to the world.

As researchers and technicians of Neuro-Linguistic Programming—that's a specific language; the language that the brain understands and responds to—we know that all humans share common traits and have similar ways of thinking (or processing information) that are preset in our brains; just like when you buy a new computer, it comes equipped with an operating system. This is called programmed by default... and you didn't even see it coming or agree to its content.

I know that you've had hopes and dreams, and that you would really love to get started on making them a reality for you. So let's get started in teaching you how you can create the life you want, by using life design methods that I will teach you when we meet, or you can start through these pages.

Starting right now, I am going to teach you how to create that life you would design if you knew how. And you will learn and begin to do it for yourself starting right now.

One client said to me at the conclusion of our second session (which was about clearing away the past negative memories), where we installed a few new beliefs, "You've made me a very happy woman."

Truly, she did all the work, because I simply guided her through a process, a means to have a realization and accept a new belief. Her happy, true, inner-self had been hiding for so long, under protective and self-limiting layers of fears and beliefs that were so outdated and no longer served her in life; she was able to discover her true happiness that she had always been hiding within.

Realistically, in the next couple of hours of reading and doing these simple life-changing exercises, you'll learn a tremendous amount. It may not magically change your life. But, what you do with the information that you'll learn in these few hours will make you a happier, healthier, even wealthier human being in so many ways.

You can truly get started in Sculpting your Life into Your Masterpiece.

In the next couple of hours you'll discover the right highway to take to get you to your destination. And if you need a little assistance along your pathway to greatness, simply contact us at the website below and either I or one of my hand-picked associates will guide you through the steps that you need to take, in order to attain the realization of your magnificent potential. In a couple of hours you will know how your mind works, and how you can begin now to Create Your Masterpiece. In the simplest language, and the most effective way, you'll learn this amazing mind training skill.

I wish for you many creative and powerful sessions!

Remember that *YOU are the Michelangelo of your own life; the David you're sculpting is YOU.*

Cesar Vargas, Ph.D.

Doctor of Clinical Hypnotherapy

www.YourLifeIsYourMasterpiece.com

YOUR MASTERPIECE

✦ ✦ ✦

THIS BOOK IS WRITTEN FOR those that appreciate art. Not just visual art, like paintings, but art of all types—music, poetry, literature, playwriting, and so on. In each of these mediums there are samples of absolute perfection, and to these we give the label *Masterpiece*. They are the greatest examples of that particular type of art.

Think about Leonardo da Vinci. Everyone knows his Mona Lisa. It took years to create and traveled many miles. It is one of the great painting masterpieces the world has ever known.

In this book, you will learn to paint a masterpiece of your life. You may have begun in some areas of your life, and in others there are still blank canvases.

Each of the greatest artists looked at a medium and saw the final product before they began to paint or chisel into stone. They knew what it would look like.

You may have a sense of what your life will look like when your masterpiece is complete. It is alright if you do not have a clear vision yet, but you will. NLP is the tool and the instruments with which you can create the masterpiece of your life. It can help you make a clear image, and it will give you the tools to make that image a reality. All you need to do is to believe in your power to create whatever you want to be in life. NLP can help you fill in the gaps. Every master had a teacher or mentor that helped him or her along the way. They taught them how to paint or sculp. They gave them the skills and helped them when they needed assistance. They could provide feedback or teach them a new technique. A professional NLP Practitioner can be that teacher or mentor you need along the way.

So get your life's canvas ready. You are about to embark upon a journey into places in your life that you may have never thought possible. You will see the beauty and potential of your life, and you will begin to develop the skills needed to succeed and transform that canvas into a living work of art. All it takes is an open mind and faith in you. You already have the tools within you; NLP will unlock your potential as a master of your life and the creator of something wonderful.

Be <u>At Cause</u>

Do you live your life At Cause? Hopefully you don't live it At Effect.

Do you know the difference? Rarely in life do individuals live their lives being totally 'At Cause' and, far too many spend too much time living on the 'At Effect' side of life, simply living their lives as a response to others' emotional states, or their desires or impulses.

Being 'At Cause' means you are 100% responsible for making a decision to create what you want in your life, and from that decision you creatively achieve or direct yourself to achieve your results in the near future. Being At Cause means that you see the world as an amazing place filled with opportunities and you are moving towards whatever you want to experience in life.

If everything doesn't go the way you want, you are able to take action and explore other potential routes to achieve what you want.

Living At Cause means that you know that you have choices; yes, you have the power to make choices. Choices are related to what you do, how you do it, when, why, and how, and how you respond to others and to all events in your life.

On the other hand are those who seem to be At Effect in life. You know those people who will blame others, or blame the circumstances of life for their failures, their bad attitudes, their bad habits, or for anything and everything. When you live life At Effect, you've given up your power to others, and you are powerless and feel powerless all the time. You might recognize those feelings in the concept 'I just never feel good with my life.'

Some married men feel that they'd do better if their wives understood them better. Some business people feel that if the Economy were better, they'd be more successful. They are being At Effect.

The truly successful people... the people who are the happiest in life, live their life At Cause.

"If wishes were fishes we'd all be casting nets."

Then again, if you waited for the fishes to jump into the boat by themselves and fry themselves up for dinner, you'd better get a good Plan B.

Wishing, and hoping, and praying and dreaming—if you're waiting for other things or situations to be different than they are, or for other people to provide that for you, then you are living At Effect, and you assume that you are a victim in life—a victim of life's circumstances.

That's not true, and living life that way, is living without fun. Can you imagine yourself that way? Can you imagine how much fun you are going to be in the eyes and lives of others? How much fun is it to believe that someone or something else is responsible for the decisions that are really yours to make? That someone or something else is even vaguely responsible for your happiness or your mood changes are some of the most difficult and self-limiting behaviors, and it allows someone else to enslave you, or simply have some magical powers over you. Talk about anxiety.

Live 'At Cause'

To live life At Cause means that you have choices in your life and you can choose exactly what is right for you. This will assure you that the choice is safe for the world around you, including family, friends, and others living in your own community. And, if you get the bigger picture, the choice is safe for the entire planet.

When you live At Effect, you are always concerned about the consequences of what you do while you still are not being responsible for your actions and how they impact others, and you are not allowing them to be responsible for their own emotional wellbeing. Because you are stuck believing that you are responsible for the emotional wellbeing of another, this puts a heavy weight on your shoulders and may manifest in you having a "pain in the neck" and a lot of stress.

People who live their lives 'At Effect' are all too often living lives as a victim, not even seeing they have choices. In reality, they DO have choices and they have made the choice not to choose, but to only react to whatever comes along the path they are traveling on.

I'm Not Perfect

I've been asked if I am always 100% on target. Honestly, no—no one is; but the vast majority of my life has been properly aimed.

Through the technology of NLP and my ability to make it easy for everyone to use, I've learned how to quickly identify the times when I am living At Effect rather than At Cause.

I realize that I've always had choices, and that I've always made choices, but sometimes they were bad ones. We all do. But through the use of NLP techniques I've got the mental toolbox to get immediately refocused and back on track.

At the same time, I have the opportunity to look at other ways to improve the quality of my choices and check out other paths to reach my goals.

In the decision to make your own choices or change directions in life there are some pre-suppositions that come to mind, and these are remembered and practically applied by all that practice the NLP techniques:

'There is no failure - only feedback'

No matter what road you take you don't come to a point of failure, only the obvious, which is a sense of awareness of what has occurred. The common terminology for this awareness is *feedback.*

One of the most vital things we do in live NLP Trainings is to emphasize the importance of your life At Cause. There is a formula for happiness, which is exemplified in the illustration on the next page:

C ⟹ E

Cause   Effect

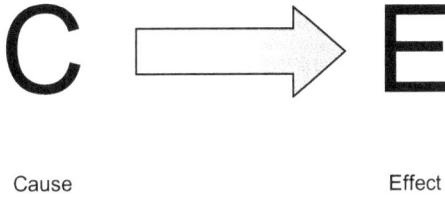

In every life situation, you're either At Cause in the equation or At Effect; you cannot be in both. Either you know that you are At Cause for absolutely everything that happens in your life, or you're At Effect.

Perhaps we could say it another way, "Take Full Responsibility" for who you are and where you are in your life right now.

An analogy for this comes from the phrase "Who's Driving Your Bus?" by NLP co-developer/creator Richard Bandler. If you think of your life as a bus ride, are you being driven around to who-knows-where, by who-knows-whom? Or, are you the bus driver, in control of the wheel and direction, and determining the speed at which you want it to happen? You can be a light touch or you could have a lead foot. Get ready!

How empowering is being At Cause? I just had a client in my office the other day. She saw her life as being totally At Effect. She had the perfect life in a Chicago suburb; she had the career, the picture-perfect family, a hard-working and loving husband, a lovely home, and life was just great. Then, her husband was transferred to California, and her entire family was uprooted and moved west.

Soon, the husband was working and was transferred yet again to Nevada, and her daughters went off to college. Now she was all alone. She had an empty-nest and a husband who wasn't physically there. As I was listening to her, I could detect "victim" language (*he* made me; *I had no choice*; *they* moved away to college) telling me that she was living her life At Effect.

As I was explaining the simple Cause and Effect formula for happiness in life, a shift began to take place inside. I could see the signs of change in her and, at the end of her session; she was ready to live a more empowered *At Cause* life.

So, which side is more empowering to you? The Cause side or the Effect side? Which is more satisfying for you? Do you find it easier to be told how to live your life, or do you want to take back that control? If you look closely enough, you will realize that the 'effects' side will lead to an unsatisfied life.

Imagine that you are in your 90's. See yourself talking to a young relative and tell them about your regrets. Tell them about all the things you wanted to do in life but have tons of reasons why you did not do them. How does that make you feel? If you went through your life with no excuses and regrets, how much more satisfying of a life would that be?

Many people in modern society are perfectly happy giving away their life to other people and circumstances. Their life becomes something that "just happened to them." They have chosen the Effects side of life. They spend their life complaining about their circumstances and blame others for putting them there. They take absolutely no responsibility for their actions and for where they are in their lives. They are the victims of circumstances and they state that they were never given a chance to do any better.

We are bombarded with messages every single day that encourage us to live life At Effect. Have you ever seen billboards or ads on public transportation, or even on the television, that start by saying, "Are you a victim? Have you been hurt by another? You need to be taken care of and others can pay your bills. It is not your fault that you have been injured. Call The John Doe Law Office today."

The message is that if you are hurt or something happened in your life, it is obviously someone else's fault and they need to pay. This is the reason doctor's visits cost so much and that healthcare costs have gone through the roof—malpractice insurance. The message of the day is that if a doctor cannot fix you, you are then entitled to sue them for malpractice. Doctors become afraid and every patient becomes a potential lawsuit. Everyone becomes a victim and lives life At Effect.

The famous baseball player Yogi Berra once said: "I never blame myself when I'm hitting bad. I just blame the bat and, if it keeps up, I change bats. After all, if I know it isn't my fault that I'm not hitting, how can I get mad at myself?"

In Yogi's case, as it is with many people, it is not the bat that is the issue. Many people blame *their own bat* for the problems they are having—the bat can be their boss, their spouse, their parents, the meter maid, and the list goes on. Do you know people like this? They say that they could be rich or successful or have what others have if only their "bat" worked properly. It is never their fault—it's the bat's fault.

As with the client I mentioned earlier, one of the things I do is help people learn through their language whether they are living their lives At Cause or At Effect. Once they can discover this for themselves, then real and profound change can start to occur. The answer and power is within all of us to change. It is amazing how we forget we have this power or simply give it away.

We live in some pretty tough times, and you may hear many people say that they are not selling enough, and that it is because of the economy. Then, how is it that some people continue to be successful even during a downturn in the economy? Is it luck or is it because they are living their life At Cause?

Consider the man that is having marital problems and blames his temper on his wife. He may say that if only she acted a certain way that he could maintain his cool. If only she did things the right way and did not argue with him he could control his temper. It could be that she just looks at him 'the wrong way' causing him to lose his temper. Is this being At Cause or At Effect?

I have known schoolteachers that place the problems they are having in the classroom on the children. They complain that the low test scores in their class are because they put all of the bad kids in their class. What about the other classes these kids are in? Why are they succeeding there? Is it really the kids that are at the heart of the problem? When did the teacher hand control over to the children? These teachers complain that the children never listen, and that is why they are not doing well in their particular class.

The blame game is the lifeblood of the person that lives their life At Effect. It is their answer to everything they are not succeeding in and it is their way of explaining why they are not reaching goals in their lives and why they are not doing what they really want to do. They are too poor, uneducated, had a bad upbringing, live in the bad part of town, attract losers... the excuses are endless.

The other day I was conversing with my friend don Miguel Ruiz, author of The Four Agreements, and he said that we all are experts... we're experts in what we repeatedly do. So, there are expert lawyers, expert mechanics, expert students, etc., just as there are experts in complaints, experts in sadness for no apparent reason, expert bickerers, and even excuses experts... experts in living At Effect.

Once a person determines that they are living their life At Effect, NLP can help you to move to the At Cause side of life. You will find that once you can move to this empowering side, you will take the driver's seat and nothing will stand in your way. You will be recreating your entire existence. NLP is the vehicle, but you remain the driver. I can help you find the driver's seat and stay there. As long as a person remains At Effect, they can never steer their life. Someone else is always driving and they remain a passenger in the back.

THERE IS A BETTER WAY TO LIVE YOUR LIFE,

AND YOU'RE ON THE RIGHT PATH.

Who Are You?

This is where we begin to look at that vision that you will need to have in order to begin to create your masterpiece of a life. Soon we're going to move forward into the concept of creating the life you desire, by design, and how to create the ideal life. But, before you can accomplish this, you need to know where you are right now.

In order to get from point A to point B, you need to know the starting point (A) and where it is located. If we were going from Los Angeles to Paris by private plane, the first thing we'd need is a flight plan—beginning with where we are taking off from, so we know precisely which route is the most efficient way to get to The City of Lights.

With reflecting on yourself and where you want to go with your life, first you need to know who you are. So, who are you?

We're going to do Exercise #1 now and your preparation is:

1. Take out a few pieces of paper.

This is regarding who you are at this moment in your life.

2. Grab paper and pen and begin writing a description of yourself in as many areas of your life as you can think of. Don't make it in outline form or write complex edited pages; you're not trying to write an autobiography, nor are you trying to impress anyone by what you're writing. Just be honest with yourself and write down on paper where you are, right now—your present reality.

3. Write about your present life, and your own present outlook on life.

4. Be sure to have at least one sheet of paper to cover each of the following areas of life:

Time	Fear
Money	Confidence/Esteem
Failure	Self-Power
Success	

Since this is going to be free-flowing associative writing, don't even think about correcting anything… just get your thoughts to flow freely about that particular subject and you. You must keep writing for at least 10 minutes, and for as long as you want. So, now start writing about you and Time, and continue writing for at least 10 minutes. Go ahead. Do it now!

Next, go on to Money, Failure, Success, Fear, Confidence/Esteem, Self-Power. Pour your thoughts onto the pages about each specific subject on different sheets of paper. When you have written on these subjects, think about what we've missed, perhaps health, physical exercise, meditation, and do the same exact writing assignment.

When this is complete – you have a far better understanding of yourself than you have ever had before. You know who you are and where you are right now in your life at this point in time.

Let us start on the path of creatively designing the life you really want, and in order to do this we need to understand the concept of a map. This may be one of the new things that you are going to learn in our great journey together. You can't get to where you want to be if you don't have a road map to get there.

But before we work together to create that great road map to your ideal future, you will need to understand a few things about how your mind works. In the field of Neuro-Linguistic Programming we are always referring to the mind and using the language itself to communicate with the mind. This is unlike the field of hypnosis, à la Milton Erickson and many others, who work to program the desired effects into the subconscious mind to be the catalyst for amazing powerful changes. NLP works similarly, but differently, at a different level and with a different language.

In order to make this concept easier, we're going to simplify this even further, so that whether you know NLP, hypnosis, meditation, or any other method, this will guide you to achieve the success that you desire. You will do this by learning a few things about how your own mind works. These concepts may be entirely new to you.

In your understanding of what you're learning, you'll realize some simple truths; be sure not to dismiss these things because of their simplicity. The power of these principles and truths resides in their simplicity and effectiveness.

*Y*OUR BRAIN IS A WOMB-TO-TOMB LEARNING MACHINE

✦ ✦ ✦

THE CONSUMMATE UNDERSTANDING OF THE MIND comes from knowing that your brain is like a computerized, automated learning machine that is always, always, always learning, absorbing information, processing it, storing it, from the moment you are born (or perhaps before) until the moment you die (or perhaps longer).

Everything that you've ever experienced is processed by your brain through at least one of your five senses. Those five senses (sight, hearing, smell, touch, and taste) create your window to the world.

Whenever you experience anything, images, sounds, smells, flavors and tactile feelings from touch or sensations related to that experience, are stored in your unconscious (subconscious) mind forever. But that's not all there is to it.

There is still one more component to consider in your experience of life. That relates to what you say to yourself, your inner-dialogue, what you think *about* those images, sounds, smells, flavors and sensations. What you think and feel about those sensations and what they mean to you, impact your life! And all of these judgments are based on your own prior experience, and your interpretation of that experience.

In effect, I am describing a machine that takes in data, analyzes it, and processes it, and modifies its own programmed reaction to it. You are a learning machine, and your Brain is the Central Processing Unit for that information. And, because of this amazing system of learning that is occurring, you are always learning, evaluating, reassessing and reinterpreting what occurs in your life, based on past experience.

If you were to look back at your life, and discover that part of it—or a significant portion of it—contains events that you weren't exactly happy to remember, those experiences or events could be catalogued in a way to "demonstrate" that *life sucks* or something more specific, *I hate men* for example.

NLP calls this self-talk the auditory-digital channel.

There are six pathways or avenues, the 5 senses plus our thoughts (or self-talk), by which data is stored in your unconscious for each experience or event in your life. Self-talk is vital in helping create the life you want because it is interrelated with the other five pathways. This is living proof that it's not solely those occurrences in your life that matter, but it's *your interpretation* of the memories of those occurrences which creates your deeply-ingrained memory of that experience and your later reactions in life, based on that memory.

POSITIVE VS. NEGATIVE SELF-TALK

Self-talk can be good and positive, but unfortunately much of it is negative and irrationally self-destructive. And that's why it's so important that you rein in control of your self-talk, and feed only the most positive of self-talk into your unconscious in various ways.

Let's look at it this way. Marci Shimoff, New York Times best-selling author of *Happy for No Reason*, estimated that the average human being was exposed to about eighty thousand thoughts a day, and about 85 percent of those were negative. In a recent presentation Marci gave, she mentioned that children heard the word 'no' thousands of times more often than the word 'yes.' Perhaps they heard the words 'no, don't, or never' do this or that too much, and not enough, 'yes, you can do it, you did great!'

That type of input from our parents and other adults in our lives usually results in some self-restriction. Or if the environment of early childhood development was a complete and total disaster, it could create a self-destructive personality. No matter who you are, or where you've been, the techniques you are going to learn here will make a positive and proactive impact in your life, bringing you, at least, additional happiness and success. And, as they say, the sky's the limit!

Whether you are a peaceful person, or even if you feel that your mind is totally out of control, you will benefit. But let me make this clear, because not all of your thoughts (and even feelings) are all positive—and some are self-condemning or self-destructive—you must weed that garden of thoughts and remove the ones that hurt the most first.

These negative thoughts are coming from a source. I'd like to take time to introduce that source of negative self-talk to you. When I'm talking to children I call him Mr. Babble. Mr. Babble just babbles on about your negative past experiences because he's comfortable in that zone. And if you try to have a success, Mr. Babble will surely try to get in the way by saying, "Why put in the extra effort, you never win; remember your older brother called you 'loser', remember the time that ...." And by the end of you *trying* to have an accomplishment, you are convinced by Mr. Babble to give up. Sometimes Mr. Babble tells you that you aren't a good person, and even insults you. Okay, you're not a kid anymore. It's time to kick Mr. Babble out of your life, now.

A while ago I heard a good perspective to this problem: "If your best friend talked to you like you allow Mr. Babble to talk to you (inside your head) you would kick the living !@#$%$ out of him?"

So, why in the world do you tolerate your own thoughts, or Mr. Babble, talking with you in that horrible manner and, to come right down to it——why do you keep talking to yourself like that?

If you realize this, you'll learn a great deal in one simple concept:

> *Thoughts become words.*
> *Words become actions.*
> *Actions become habits.*
> *Habits become your character.*
> *Character becomes your destiny.*

Lesson: As best as you can, choose your thoughts well. And, in reality, you are the person who must weed the garden of thoughts, although sometimes you may wonder if you are weeding it well. Well, if you are a good farmer, you will have phenomenally huge flowers, veggies and fruits growing with none of the other crap in life. You've gotten rid of all the weeds and now the seeds that you have sown have blossomed in a field of colors, and delectable fruits, vegetables, and grains that bring health and energy to your life and make you come alive. That gives you sufficient motivation to be a good thought farmer, doesn't it?

MENTAL FILTERS: DELETIONS, DISTORTIONS, GENERALIZATIONS, MAPS OF THE WORLD

◆ ◆ ◆

Think of all the beauty that's still left in and around you and be happy!

Anne Frank

INFORMATION IS COMING AT US at a rate of over two million bits per second through our senses. Our mind can only process a tiny portion of that information and so there are filters that help in the process. Some of the information that our mind does not deem necessary is deleted; our mind distorts some of the information that does not match our expectations and internal programming; and, finally, it generalizes things to make it simpler to digest and process.

Each of us is unique in that we see and experience the world through a unique set of filters. We are also unique because our mind interprets the information coming from our senses. Two people can look at the same scene at the same time and have two totally different experiences. In NLP, this is referred to as *maps of the world*. For instance, two people can watch a movie about dogs. One person may cry because it reminded him about a dog that he had when he was a little boy and he misses his dog. The other person might hate the movie because when he was small he was attacked by Rottweiler. Through the life experiences that each of us have, we develop *mental filters* and "Meta Programs."

These Meta Programs affect a person's thought processing and decision-making abilities. They do not reflect personality types; rather, they are all about how your subconscious mind filters information and how this impacts your behavior and reactions. These filters often dictate how you run your life. Meta Programs are one of the reasons why we live At Cause or At Effect. The Meta Programs dictate whether we look for results or reasons.

There are a number of different filters that are accessed depending on the situation and the sensory data that is being presented. You can notice these filters being activated based on your own self-talk. When you think a certain way, express your feelings or act according to repetitive behaviors, it is due to these Meta Programs.

Here are some Meta Programs to consider:

Options vs. Procedures: Do you make your decisions based on options or procedures? If you are not sure, here is an example:

Suppose I asked you, "How did you decide what outfit to wear to a work function?"

If you operate under a Procedures filter you might say: "I asked the boss what I needed to wear. I looked at how other people were dressed and looked at the work manual to see what the dress code was." In this instance, you were looking for the proper procedure for making your decision. Remember, this is not a personality type, but it is a program that has been set up in your mind in order to make decisions. A procedure filter is often chronological in nature; you might say, "First I do this, then I do that… followed by doing something else."

If you operate under an Options filter you might say:

"I really want to buy an outfit for this function. I really like the browns I have seen people wearing this season. I am not sure brown is the right color for a nighttime function. I have wanted a certain outfit at the store; maybe it is on sale."

This filter is the opposite of the procedures filter. It is not in any order and, in fact, people with this type of filter avoid procedures. There is no judgment about which type of filter is right or wrong; it is just important to recognize the type of filters under which you operate.

In NLP work, I am able to expose these filters and help the person decide whether they are working for them or not. Do these filters push them more toward living At Cause or living At Effect?

Another type of filter is "**Standards.**" Some people look internally for standards while others look externally for answers. People with an internal Standards filter, figure things out on their own. They are not swayed by external advice or opinions. They must figure things out for themselves and experience them first hand. Reading or hearing about something is not enough. In fact, their filter will often make them reject outside opinions or direction.

On the other hand, people with external filters, look for what others are saying and doing. They do not trust their own instincts and often challenge their own thinking and ideas. These people tend to look for others to tell them what to do. These people tend to live more At Effect rather than At Cause.

If you are not sure which type of filter you might be using, consider the following question:

"How do you know if you did a good job at work?"

People with an external type filter might say: "I was told that I did a good job. The results were as other people expected. I asked my coworkers and boss how they thought I was doing. I either got a raise or did not. If I did not get a raise then I did not do a good job."

As you might notice, all of the reasons were external. They are seeking data to support the question. This data is from outside sources. So let us consider the person with the internal filter:

"I just know I did a good job. I set goals for myself and I met them. It does not matter what other people say, I am a hard worker that gets results."

As you see, this type of person is setting the standards internally. They are not looking for outside verification from others. They set internal goals and met them. They did not need someone telling them they did a good job, and even if they did tell them they did a bad job, the person with the Internal Standards filter will make up their own mind as to whether they did or not.

These filters are not black and white. They are neither good nor bad. In some cases, one may be preferred over another, but it is the results of the decision-making that are important. These filters comprise a scale, and most of us can be found along this scale somewhere. Each situation may elicit a slightly different Meta Program; however, we are usually more than one type (i.e., more internal than external) than another. Working with NLP processes can create new filters and Meta Programs that are more suited to gaining success in life. As we switch from Effect to Cause, new programs are created while others are deleted.

Sometimes these Meta Programs can lead to deletions, distortions and mental errors. Meta Programs become our maps of the world. They are how we view ourselves and how we navigate our lives. These programs exist in our unconscious, although our thoughts and decisions are filtered through them. Sometimes important information is caught in these filters and therefore is not considered. They can distort our worldview and can lead to a negative view of our world and our lives.

Let us consider some of these Meta Programs that can lead to distortion. In understanding and identifying them, you can use NLP to reprogram them. Here are some faulty thought patterns that you can identify and modify in order to change your life. Do not feel guilty or have any more negative thoughts about it.

Just accept that they exist and then realize you can make definite changes. The power is within you. Each thought error starts with an example.

> **All-or-Nothing Thought Error:** Susan put her bid in for a promotion in her area at work. Unfortunately they hired someone else for the position that had been with the company much longer and had more specialized experience. Susan feels down and thinks she will never be promoted. She feels that her career is a total failure. This type of thought error uses words like *never, forever,* and *always.* Every situation seems to be absolute. They do not think in gray areas—it is always black or white. There are no exceptions, and situations are filtered through *always* and *never.*

One of the ways to manage this type of thought error is to remove *always*, *never* and *forever* from your vocabulary. A NLP Coach can help you with this. A new type of self-talk has to occur to eliminate this error. This type of thought error can land a person in the Effect side of life. Everything becomes an absolute and therefore they are always in the role of a victim. Here is an example of how self-talk can be changed in this situation, and how Susan could have coped with not getting that promotion:

"I really wanted the promotion, but someone else that has more experience got the job. This does not mean I was a failure; it just means that they picked the right person for the job, at this time. I am still really good at what I do and will work on improving my skills and looking for opportunities to gain more experience so that the next time a position becomes open I will be ready. Just because I had one tiny setback does not mean I am a failure. It is an opportunity to improve. I am a great employee and will continue to improve my skills."

Overgeneralization: Kelly does not interact with people often. She had a couple of bad relationships and now when friends ask her out to dinner, she refuses. She does not see any reason to go out because others don't like her. There is no use in trying because people will just use and hurt her.

When there is an overgeneralization error, people will take one or two isolated incidents and make them the rule for their life. If one person is mean, then everyone is mean. If they failed to pass a test, then they will fail all tests. Is it true *everyone* is out to hurt Kelly?

Are *all* people just mean? Kelly has friends that are asking her out to have a good time, are they just asking her so they can use her and be mean to her? Obviously they care about Kelly, but she acts based on the isolated incidents, and comes to the conclusion—through an overgeneralization—that everyone will do the same thing to her.

It is natural to over generalize, at times, especially if you are emotional about something. When you sense you might be over generalizing, remember that even though groups of people have things in common, they are still made up of individuals who are unique. No one is exactly the same as anyone else. Even if you might come across mean and nasty people, this does not mean that *everyone* is mean and nasty.

Even if you have a bad experience with one person or a group of people, do your best not to let that experience make you over generalize about the situation or the people involved. One bad apple does not mean every other apple is rotten. Do not allow one rotten apple to spoil the whole barrel for you. See it for what it truly is—a personalized, individual learning experience.

You can miss opportunities that will lead you to the life you desire. NLP is a great way to remove overgeneralizations. An NLP coach or trainer can challenge these over generalized *always*, *never* and *forever* statements. They can even help you replace this Meta Program with one that is more flexible and allows you to see individual incidents and people for what they truly are without it ruining your world view.

Deletion Thought Error: Jim is having a particularly rotten day. As he is driving home, someone almost runs him off the road. Jim's self-talk is about how all drivers are rude and that the town he lives in is full of rude people. As he continues, he almost runs into another car as they cut him off. This reinforces the idea that all the drivers are nasty people that should have their licenses revoked. Jim tries to switch lanes and someone stops and motions them with a hand gesture and a smile. Jim pulls into the lane and ignores the smile and the gesture. He is still angry about the two times he was cut off and still thinks the town is full of rude and dangerous drivers.

Mental deletion is the process of only concentrating on bad events and missing the good ones when they occur. This mindset of Effect only recognizes bad events and deletes the rest. This mental deletion singles out negative thoughts and events and walks right by positive ones when they occur. People become blinded to the positive events and people in their lives.

Looking for the positive things that occur, and looking for the silver lining in every storm cloud can help you to overcome this type of mental error. This can take some practice and guidance, and an NLP tutor can be invaluable now. They can help reset the program to look for positive things and events and focus on them. Jim could have had a different outlook on the town and its drivers if he had paid attention to the person waving at him and being a courteous driver. Sometimes it can take some searching, but NLP makes this search much easier to do.

Disqualifying the Positive: Katherine recently bought a new dress. Her friends tell her she looks fantastic in it, but Katherine says she looks fat and it does not fit right. She says that clothes never make her look good and this dress is an example of that.

People that live life At Effect are experts at turning positive things into negative ones. They play the part of the victim well, and will not allow positive compliments to ruin that. Sometimes this can be because of low self-esteem, but it is still a filter and therefore it can be reprogrammed using NLP techniques.

People that disqualify the positive sometimes feel like they do not deserve the compliment, so they turn it into a negative, or discount it. In order to change it, the person must learn to smile and say *thank you*. This is a reprogramming from the automatic response of turning it negative. The more this is practiced along with other NLP techniques, the easier it is to remove this filter.

Jumping to Conclusions: Sam has a dinner date with his girlfriend. She is late and he cannot reach her by phone. He assumes that she does not care, may be with another man or that the relationship is over. His date is simply stuck in traffic because of an accident and her cell phone battery is dead. There is no way she can contact Sam.

Another way to look at this thought error is that this filter makes us always assume the worst. It is, again, about self-esteem, self-worth and faulty thinking. This kind of filter may have been created by some isolated incidents, but instead of waiting to hear the true explanation or assuming that the situation is less negative, this type of filter makes us jump to, often, the wrong conclusion.

When Sam's girlfriend arrived and explained what happened, was it worth the lamenting and worry? Of course not! Was it necessary for Sam to think the worst? No! Often in these situations Sam might even be angry when his date arrives and ruin the evening because of false assumptions that are often based on very little, if any, solid data.

The way to deal with this type of thought error is to think positively about the person and give them the benefit of the doubt. Did they ever give you a reason not to trust them? They are dating you so obviously they care about you. Are you making assumptions because of some other person? Are you truly giving the person a chance? NLP helps reshape these types of snap judgments about people and situations.

Magnification and Minimization: Todd has been preparing for the big soccer game at the end of the week. He has been practicing hours a day for months. He makes the winning goal with a skilled shot. His teammates pat him on the back and congratulate him on his skill. He states that he was just lucky and that he should have played better so that it would not have come down to one goal.

Another example is that Judy forgot to clock in at her work. Her boss reminds her that she needs to do this every day. He gives her this feedback in a calm manner with a smile. Judy begins crying and stating she can't do anything right and that her boss would have every right to fire her immediately.

This first example is that of minimizing a situation. Todd worked hard to achieve that goal but he made it no big deal and then proceeded to make it his fault and that he really did not play as well as others were saying.

This mental filter makes things small and insignificant. Nothing is ever good enough. This is not to be confused with humility because this error always makes the person a victim, no matter what they accomplish.

The second example is totally on the other end of the spectrum. This mental error makes mountains out of molehills. Everything is larger-than-life and the biggest catastrophe. Small things are blown way out of proportion, and even the smallest feedback is the end of the world.

Think of this filter as being like a telescope. When you look through one end everything is bigger-than-life and magnified, but if you turn it around everything looks tiny.

The best way to deal with this sort of filter is to back away from the situation. See the forest through the trees. By using NLP, you will be able to put things in perspective. You will be able accept small mistakes as learning experiences, and move on without blowing things out of proportion.

Emotional Reasoning: Laura looks at the pile of work on her desk after a vacation. It seems so large that she is overwhelmed. She feels like it will be hopeless and she will never catch up.

Laura has based her assessment of the situation on how it makes her *feel* not how it really is. It may make her feel bad to think of the large task ahead of her, but is it really hopeless? In reality, cleaning her desk is a doable task. She just doesn't feel up to it. She has reached the conclusion that it is useless to try based on the fact that it overwhelms her.

One way to overcome this filter is to break down large tasks into smaller ones. Once you have broken it down into smaller pieces, list them in the order of importance. As you go down your list, begin to check them off. As you begin to make progress, the feelings of being overwhelmed start to vanish. Rather than being paralyzed, doing small things toward your goal will help undo this filter. NLP can help reprogram this filter so that when you look at a large task you automatically begin to break it down.

'Should' Statements: Justin is sitting in a busy restaurant. He has been sitting for five minutes, and thinks that the waiter should have already taken his drink order and brought it to him. Later he was waiting for his meal and thinks that it should have already been brought to him. These thoughts make the dinner not as enjoyable because of the reoccurring thoughts about what should or should not be happening.

Things do not always occur the way we think they should. This Meta Program can cause problems in a relationship, because one person is always stating what the other person should be doing, saying or thinking. When things do not occur the way the person feels that they should, it could lead to irritation and anxiety.

To overcome this, NLP allows the person to release things and let things go. They can learn that even though they have the power to create their own reality, it does not mean that they can control every action or event that occurs in their life; all they can do is control how they react and deal with it.

Labeling and Mislabeling: A healthy person is receiving help from social services and therefore they are lazy and do not want to work.

The Labeling Meta Program can be a destructive one, because it limits a person's ability to grow and achieve their life's goals. Creating labels makes us react to others in negative ways, at times. If we label ourselves, then we will become whatever that label says we are—not good enough, lazy, lack will power, etc... NLP will erase and rewrite the Labeling Meta Program. Good labels can be effective—strong, smart, motivated—so these new programs and filters can be useful in retraining our minds for success.

Projection: Sarah's son got into trouble at school and was suspended. Sarah feels that it is her fault that her son made bad choices and feels that she is a bad mother.

Projection is a common Meta Program people run, especially on the Effect side of the equation. They take responsibility for things that are not their fault. It feeds the victim mentality and allows them to state that their life is bad, and use other people's bad decisions as evidence that they are to blame, in some way. Part of the shift to living At Cause is personal responsibility. It is not only about taking personal responsibility for your life, but it is also allowing others to take responsibility for their own. Sarah is not to blame for her son's bad decisions and therefore she does not need to take that on to herself. Sarah can be the best mother in the world, and still her son could make a bad decision, because he is an individual person, not a robot.

One way to reprogram this Meta Program is to consider this. Suppose Sarah's son made the basketball team. He worked hard, practiced and succeeded on his own. Sarah would not necessarily take all the credit for that, so why would she take the blame if he did not make the team or made a bad decision that landed him in suspension.

Each of the Meta Programs and filters that we use as maps to the world are common and, again, you should not feel guilty if you recognize some of yourself in these examples. You may have one or two of these filters working at any time. Be happy that you can recognize them, because this is the first step in reprogramming them. Sometimes, it can be difficult to overcome these filters on your own. It can take an outside person, like an NLP Practitioner, to help you through the process. They can help you challenge negative thoughts and assist in creating new programs designed just for you to create new Meta Programs and therefore shift your life toward living At Cause and also making your map of the world much brighter and brimming with possibility.

Happiness is not a matter of events; it depends upon the tides of the mind.

Alice Meynell

PRIME DIRECTIVES
OF THE UNCONSCIOUS
MIND

✦ ✦ ✦

OUR CONSCIOUS MIND HAS A QUIETER PARTNER—the powerful counterpart that is called the unconscious mind. It is the unconscious mind, and the profound power within, that NLP really targets, as that is where all change occurs. Let's first look at what the unconscious mind is.

By definition, the unconscious is the part of our mind that you are simply not aware of. It exists to perform the automatic functions of the mind and, while we are not always aware of it, it is always awake, and it is always working. It is this part of the mind that NLP works with, because it manages our memories, habits and instincts.

The unconscious mind has a number of jobs, or prime directives, that it is responsible for. It performs its duties without either complaint or conscious thought on our part. It is constantly working so that we can function normally and at our best. NLP suggestions that follow along on the same pathway as these prime directives are more likely to be received and integrated into our unconscious. Let us look at these 20 Prime Directives and what they mean to our body's and our mind's wellbeing.

Prime Directives of the Unconscious Mind:

1. The Unconscious Mind stores memories

All of your memories are stored in the unconscious mind. It stores them in two main ways—temporal and atemporal. Temporal memory has to do with the way a memory is associated with time. These are scenes of childhood that you can remember like mini-mind movies. These memories move in time through your mind when you recall them. You also have a sense of when these memories occurred because of their relation to different memories. You can easily tell if a memory was from childhood or when you were 23.

The next type of memory is atemporal, which means it has no relationship to time. For instance, you can remember the word "elephant". You learned it sometime and know what it means, but it has no relationship to a temporal event. When you read it you remember what it means and you can say and write the word. This is an atemporal memory, which refers to a general memory, not fixed on any time line. That is different from a temporal memory of when you saw an elephant at a zoo when you were 10 years old, for instance. This is, actually, a temporal event.

The mind creates both temporal and atemporal memories, without any effort whatsoever of our conscious mind. In fact, the unconscious can even create memories from dreams.

2. The Unconscious Mind is the domain of the emotions

Human beings, for the most part, are emotional beings. All emotions begin and are stored in the unconscious mind. We may experience them with our conscious mind, but have you ever tried to force yourself to be happy or sad or even angry? You cannot tell yourself, "I am going to be mad now." And then experience that emotion, unless you are trained in acting or watch a heck of a lot of movies or TV.

You might think about things that make you angry and those thoughts and memories might already exist in your unconscious mind and it would then be easier for you to access those feelings.

These emotions live and are generated in the unconscious when certain stimuli are presented, which can evoke memories from the past that are stored in the unconscious.

3. The Unconscious organizes all your memories

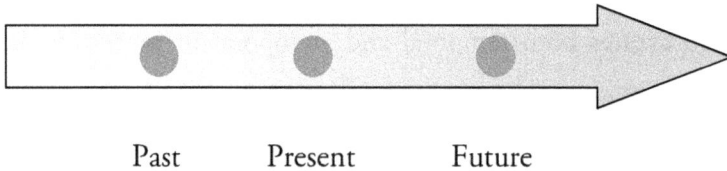

Past   Present   Future

For the temporal memories, it is best to use a time line. It puts memories in order. It also organizes memories using the mechanics of Gestalt[1] grouping. This type of memory grouping creates chains of meaningful memories based upon subject, meaning or feelings. It allows for the recall of memories to be easier through association. Consider the color "blue." There are blue birds, blueberries, the blue color of the walls of your childhood home, the blue color of the sky; the list is endless, but they can all be grouped together under the concept of *blue.*

This is important in NLP because sometimes these pairings and groupings can be a bit less positive than we'd like; in fact, they can be outright negative. Sometimes we may make incorrect judgments about people and events because of how our mind associates things and events. This grouping is also responsible for how our phobias are formed.

One bad event can affect our response to similar events in the future.

For instance, a dog may have bitten you when you were little. Therefore, whenever you see a dog it may make you apprehensive. You may not even know the reason why. Because of this possible association, you may be scared of all animals that are furry like dogs. You may not like fur or even the color of fur because of the association you created unconsciously. These negative groupings and associations can be easily undone by NLP.

4. The Unconscious Mind represses memories with unresolved negative emotion.

There is a likelihood that some events may have been suppressed into the unconscious because the memory was too difficult to deal with or manage at the time. The memories may have been overwhelming. In the Hawaiian tradition of Huna they describe this as a 'little black bag' that is shoved down within us. Sometimes, these memories simply bubble up and surface while you are walking, when out of the blue some memory jumps out at you. At that instant, we have two choices:

a. we can either address the situation or

b. we can repress it again.

Sometimes these emotions can be trapped in different areas of the body. "Boy, my boss is giving me a pain in the neck." Or, "I can't stand how my wife and I keep fighting." Both of these thoughts are absolutely dangerous and can cause a Meta Program to be running out of control.

These trapped emotions can be released through bodywork like massage. It is not uncommon for people to experience a release of emotions and memories when parts of the body are massaged.

Memories come up and, if they talk about them, emotional pain can be released promptly, without further effects in the future.

5. The Unconscious Mind presents to you your repressed memories for resolution.

Even though the unconscious mind represses some memories, it also has a prime directive to bring them up for possible resolution. It brings up these memories and tries to make them rational. It does this by releasing negatives from those memories until the memory no longer bothers you. Once it has been resolved or desensitized, the memories no longer need to be repressed and you can comfortably live with them at the conscious mind level.

6. The Unconscious Mind may continue to repress emotions for self-protection.

There are some events that are so traumatic that the mind pushes them so far down that they cannot be accessed in conventional ways. NLP can often release these memories that create blocks in our lives, even if we don't know they exist. The unconscious suppresses these so deeply because they are just too painful for our conscious mind to look at and deal with.

7. The Unconscious Mind runs the body

The Unconscious Mind has two blueprints of the body. One is the way the body is now and the other is the body in perfect health, which is stored in the deepest part of the unconscious mind, which may also be called your higher self. The unconscious regulates all your involuntary functions such as your heartbeat, breathing, and digestion. These things are not in the realm of the conscious mind. You might think that breathing can be controlled but actually conscious breathing is different than automatic breathing.

Some people may wonder whether they can truly trust their unconscious mind. Ask yourself this question: "What takes care of breathing while you are sleeping? Does your heart not keep beating?" Your unconscious mind controls all of these functions whether we are asleep or awake.

8. The Unconscious Mind preserves the body

The unconscious mind is in charge of maintaining the integrity of the body condition and keeping it active and well. Sometimes the unconscious forgets this directive, and disease might occur or you might get sick or have pain just so the unconscious can get your attention. These symptoms are really messages that the unconscious is having difficulty getting to your conscious mind level to receive and act upon.

When you are stressed, for example, you may begin to develop joint and back pain. This is often a message sent to you from within that you need to slow down and take care of yourself. This is beautifully explained by my good friend Karol K. Truman in her book *Feelings Buried Alive, Never Die*, where she delves into detail about where this dis-ease comes from and, more importantly, how to deal with it in an easy and effective way.

9. The Unconscious Mind is a highly moral being

The type of morality is not the kind imposed by religion, society or doctrines. It is the morality you were taught and accepted. These are the standards and ideals you have chosen to live by. Your unconscious mind abides by these morals and acts according to what they dictate, even when you're in a deep hypnotic state. You always have this protection.

When some people consult with me for private Hypnosis or Neuro-Linguistic Programming sessions, they may have a fear that they may be made to do something they don't want to do, such as reveal "all their secrets." Because of this prime directive, you can rest assured knowing that your unconscious mind will protect you, and won't allow you to do anything that goes against your moral code, that is, the moral code that you were taught and accepted.

10. The Unconscious Mind enjoys serving

The difficulty is that the unconscious needs clear orders to follow. Many people give inconsistent directions to their unconscious mind. One day they may say to themselves that they are smart and the next they say that are dumb. These statements are the ones that the unconscious mind follows; these mixed messages only confuse the unconscious mind and, therefore, its functionality can be chaotic. For best results, the Unconscious Mind requires constant, consistent, and clear directions.

In my workshops, I use the example of our unconscious mind being like a 5-year-old genie. The genie has the power to give you what you want and, when you make your request, his response is always, "Your wish is my command." Your unconscious mind will give you everything you ask for, but you must tell it exactly what you want, clearly and unequivocally.

11. The Unconscious Mind controls and maintains all perceptions

As data from your senses comes into your brain, it is your unconscious mind that receives and filters the information. The unconscious mind receives and transmits perceptions to the conscious mind. Therefore, if a person needs help with perceptions (like problems with their hearing or eyesight); it is best worked with through the unconscious mind. NLP is very well suited to help enhance these perceptions.

12. The Unconscious Mind generates, stores, distributes and transmits "energy"

Your mind, body and, especially, your nervous system operate on electrical energy. Signals from your senses are transmitted through energy channels. Life itself is energy. This energy is regulated by the unconscious mind. When your body is feeling sluggish and needs more energy, your unconscious mind can help give your body and mind more energy. Sometimes a person can be afflicted with diseases such as the Epstein Barr virus, which can sap the body of energy. Through NLP and communication with the unconscious mind, this energy can be easily restored.

13. The Unconscious Mind maintains instincts and generates habits

This is great news because by accessing your unconscious mind you can program new habits while getting rid of ones you do not want. It is like deleting old software and then uploading newer ones. The unconscious mind is ready to be programmed and to do as you command it to.

Your instincts, such as the "fight or flight" response, also reside here, so NLP can help with anxiety and other responses associated with the autonomic nervous system. The autonomic nervous system helps get the body ready for action. Sometimes this is necessary, and other times it is not. NLP can help activate the other system, the parasympathetic system, to bring your body and mind back to a state of homeostasis—calm and balance.

14. The Unconscious Mind needs repetition until a habit is installed

This means that you must repeat an action a number of times before it becomes a habit. Once that habit has been imprinted on your unconscious mind, until you somehow erase it or replace it, it remains in your life.

One of the great things about NLP is that you can accelerate this directive. Through the use of NLP techniques you can speed up the repetitions and make changes rapidly and permanently.

15. The Unconscious Mind is programmed to continually and always seek more

As humans we are programmed to look for more. We are never content with what we have; we always seek a little bit more. We seek to be better and that is how we have evolved, and continue to evolve. This drive can help us achieve great things, but sometimes it can cause problems. This drive to seek more thrills is the basis of how substance abuse works. Most of the time people with a drug addiction will start off small, with what are called "gateway drugs" and, once that is not fun anymore, they will try a harder drug and the cycle goes on and on. Many thrill seekers are driven by the unconscious to live highly risky lives and go for more and greater risks as their 'high' from the last experience fades. NLP can help take this directive and point it in the right direction that benefits the thrill-seeker.

16. The Unconscious Mind functions best as a whole integrated unit

This means that even though the unconscious mind may be complicated and appear to have many parts, it is the whole working together that is most important. Individual parts are not as important as the integrated parts, working as one unit. When your thoughts, emotions, health and life seem to be chaotic, this can be a sign that your unconscious mind is not working as a whole. NLP can help make your unconscious work efficiently, like a well-oiled machine.

17. The Unconscious Mind is symbolic

While we communicate with words, the unconscious mind communicates with symbols, images, and pictures. Psychologist Carl Jung explored the symbols of the mind and also worked with patients to interpret dreams. He felt that dreams were the way the unconscious communicates with us. We may sense symbols in our waking hours attracting our attention. It is the unconscious sending you a message. Often, these symbols are not to be interpreted literally; rather, they should be looked at metaphorically. If you see a lion in your dream, this does not mean you will be eaten by a huge feline. It can represent strength, power, leadership, virility, etc.

18. Your Unconscious Mind takes everything personally. (The basis of Perception is Projection)

You may have heard the phrase my Mom told me, *"When you point your finger at someone, three fingers are pointed at you."* Everything you say, do, and think, your unconscious mind processes and interprets to be about you. So even when you are talking about someone else, your unconscious mind interprets that you are talking about yourself. The Good News and Bad News is that everything is about you.

Everything you are saying is about you, so it is important that you are impeccably careful of what you are saying. You do not want your unconscious to get the wrong messages and begin acting on them. In his book *The Four Agreements*, Dr. Miguel Ruiz talks about being impeccable with your words; this prime directive of the unconscious mind is the reason why this first agreement is so important.

This is one of the most effective things NLP can do, and the reason why it works so well is because images, pictures, symbols have a profound effect on you and can change the input, programming and messages you are receiving in your daily life, and thus it can make a huge impact on your life.

19. The Unconscious Mind works on the principle of least effort

The Unconscious looks for the path of least resistance. This doesn't mean *laziness*; it means, more or less, simplicity in effectiveness. It's a precise system, so you must be very precise with your language. Suppose you said to yourself that this month you were going to make a lot more money. When you are walking to the bus you find a dollar on the ground and pick it up. Your unconscious could interpret that this one-dollar bill is the sum total of all the extra money you were referring to, and therefore it stops searching for the extra money.

If on the other hand, you said to you unconscious mind that you were going to make an extra $5,000 in the next two months, you will more likely to see results, as your unconscious mind would not stop until it reached that particular goal.

20. The Unconscious Mind does not process negatives

You unconscious mind cannot negate something without creating the image first. Suppose I told you not to think of a purple people eater. I would say, "No matter what you do, do not think of the large purple people eater. If you think of a purple people eater it will be bad luck for you. So whatever you do, do not think of that purple people eater."

There is no way that the unconscious mind can process this negative. The second you heard *purple people eater* the image comes into your mind. You cannot undo the image nor *not think* about it upon command.

This actually has a practical application in that pushing the mind not to think of something will actually make the mind create it. Some therapists have used this technique to guide their clients' unconscious mind to create what they want.

For example, "Before you deeply relax, I want to talk to you about imagery, so it is important that you only relax a little and do not totally relax yet. If your body becomes completely relaxed you will not hear the next part, so do not even think of totally relaxing."

The result is that the unconscious mind, in an attempt not to create a state of relaxation, will actually create it.

It is important to understand these prime directives because it is how the unconscious mind operates and it is where NLP will interface and connect with your conscious mind in order to make positive changes in your thoughts and habits, and ultimately begin to transform your life from the inside out.

This is akin to understanding color theory, positive and negative perspective, and lights and shadows when you want to create your masterpiece. Once you know and understand the principles and how they work together, you have the knowledge and the flexibility to create to your heart's content.

NLP PRESUPPOSITIONS

✦ ✦ ✦

THERE ARE SETS OF PRESUPPOSITIONS about NLP that are important to know before you get started. They are a set of powerful beliefs or assumptions we must adopt to truly understand what the purpose of NLP is. They help filter our reality in a powerful way.

NLP presuppositions help us empower ourselves as we begin to replace negative beliefs that are holding us back with ones that will open us to positive change. For instance, if you believe that you cannot change, the likelihood is that you will not. If you truly believe that you have the power to let go of old assumptions about your life, environment or condition, then this is the most likely catalyst for change.

It is important that you're familiar with these presuppositions before you come to your NLP training, and they'll also help you to deal more efficiently and productively with others in your daily life.

These presuppositions help structure and filter everything we do in NLP. They change our internal representations of the world. NLP practitioners know that they cannot produce results using NLP technology if the person truly does not believe it to be possible. These presuppositions are absolutely necessary for success in NLP. When you come to an NLP live training we will look for the implementation of these beliefs and presuppositions. They are also useful to understand others, and get along with them. Please understand that these presuppositions are not necessarily true every time and in all cases, but our work as NLP practitioners, and your results as a practitioner, a client or both, will improve dramatically when you act as if they were true. When we do, we are empowered by new beliefs, a new attitude, and a new way of looking at the world and everything in it with possibility, instead of pessimism, and with freedom instead of failure.

Let's look at these empowering presuppositions now.

1. The first presupposition is that the NLP practitioner must respect your model of the world.

This does not mean that they have to agree with your model, but they must respect and interact with it. No matter where you are in your life and no matter what you believe at the moment, the NLP practitioner must respect that, and deal with you where you truly are.

In February 2006, I received a phone call from a prospective client. He asked if I did regression work to clarify events in the past. I said *yes* and we proceeded to make the appointment. When the young man arrived at my office, he said he had had a close encounter with a UFO back in his country. He began describing the experience and how he had received a vision for the end of the world, which would be June 6, 2006, or 6/6/06. I helped him access those memories, clear them up, and he felt better after the experience.

Whether I believe in extraterrestrials or not, imagine what would have happened if I mocked him or his close encounter experience. Obviously, I would have been useless for him as an NLP Practitioner. As caring NLP Coaches, it is imperative that we respect the other person's model of the world.

This is also vital concerning your interactions with others. It's important for you to withhold judgment of others, and have respect for them as they are.

2. NLP practitioners must deal with your behavior and your change in terms of context and ecology

This means that they must help you refine your goals in two ways: The first is context. Suppose you are feeling sluggish in life and want more energy. Do you want more energy all the time? What about in the middle of the night? Do you want energy then?

You must learn to evaluate things in context and refine those desires and beliefs to make sure they are exactly what you are looking for. Your unconscious mind will give you what you ask for, so you must make sure you are very precise with what you request.

The second part is that you must study how consequences work and how they impact those around you. This is your ecology—your environment—this is where you live. This includes family, friends, co-workers, etc. Do your beliefs and goals negatively affect anyone else in your life? Are these beliefs and goals healthy for you and everyone else you come in contact with?

3. NLP practitioners must accept that any resistance in the client is a sign of lack of rapport.

If you are not connecting with your NLP practitioner or coach, there will not be much movement. This does not mean that you are resisting change; it just means that communication must be flexible. Your success is dependent upon the practitioner's ability to find the right techniques and the right approach that will work for you. For your part, it's important that you allow the process to work. Communication is a two-way street, and open communication and trust are essential in order for NLP to work.

4. People are not their behaviors

This is important for both you and your NLP coach. He must accept you for who you are and work towards change of your behaviors. You do not need to change who you are as a person; only make changes in your behavior. In reality, you'll discover that you are a wonderful and awesome person, and you bring unique gifts to the world. This does not need to be changed at all. The only areas for change would be any negative behaviors, and they need to be addressed and replaced.

If someone were to ask you 'who are you?' you might say, "I am a doctor...I am a mother... I am a lawyer..." These describe behaviors, not who you truly are. The essential point here is that you are not your label.

In fact, labels can be negative things. When you adopt a label or project a label onto someone else, it can shift his or her map of the world. Their behaviors will shift to become what the label dictates and if it is a self-limiting label, it will restrict life. For instance, if you say someone is obese, there is a lot of baggage that goes with that label. If they themselves adopt the label of obesity, it will keep them in that state simply in order to uphold and verify what that label means. They will have great difficulty losing weight and they will remain obese because they adopted that label.

5. Everyone is doing the best that they can with the resources they have available

The assumption here is twofold. One assumption is that we have a certain set of skills and resources that have been available to us during life. These resources may seem limited to some, but we cannot do better than the resources we have. NLP will increase these skills and resources multifold.

The second assumption is that, all things considered, people generally do their best in most situations. Humans are adaptable; they work toward doing their best, even if for some people's standards this may not seem like it is enough. For an NLP worker, they must engage you where you are and assume you are already trying your hardest.

This is where *forgiveness* comes in when we talk about the NLP field because, if you are doing the best you can with the resources you have available, it lets you off the hook. No matter what you are doing, there is the assumption that there is a positive intention or need behind it. It may not be the best way to go about getting it done, but it may be the best you know how to do that at that moment in time. So let yourself off the hook and realize that with NLP you'll be learning new skills and habits. And that will guide you on the path to becoming all that you can be.

6. The most important thing to focus on is what a person is doing, not what they are saying.

Everyone has a story. We can talk story (as they say in Hawaii) all day long about what we did, what we failed to do, and what we want to do. It is not what we say that is important; it is what we actually do that is important. One of the things that people will say is that they will "try" to do something. This does not mean that they will do it. In fact, the word "try" implies that there is no success likely, but that there was some effort.

'Try' this. Place you hand on the table, palm up. Place a paperclip in the palm of your hand. Now try to lift your hand. YOU DID IT! *You did not try to lift it! You did it.* Language can be very tricky, and it can really affect what we do and do not do, but it is the action that is most important.

> *"Do or do not—there is no try"*
>
> Yoda

7. The map is not the territory.

The words we use are not the event or item they represent. The words are not the events themselves; they are merely labels and representations of what we are describing. The concept to grasp here is that the map is not the actual place that it represents.

Think about the town you live in. A cartographer—a person who draws maps—may have made a great map of your town. However, the map is separate, and while it is a representation of your town, it is not the town itself. Suppose they blew up the map the size of a house and made it more detailed. While it might be a great map, it still would not be the town. Now consider if they created a map using a greatest team of cartographers ever known that was the actual size of your town. It would have every single detail and the map could be placed over your town. No matter how large or detailed a map is, it never IS the territory it represents.

I remember hearing the story of a young aristocrat in Spain who went to see Pablo Picasso and commissioned a painting of his girlfriend. When the young man went to pick up the portrait, which was painted in the Cubism style, he was aghast and said, "What is this? This is not my girlfriend! My girlfriend is beautiful and kind." So the master replied, "Then, what does your girlfriend look like?" To which the man responded by taking out a small picture from his wallet and shoving it in the hands of the Cubist. Upon deliberate contemplation of the picture, Picasso replied, "Well, she is rather tiny and flat."

Each person has their own map of what their world is to them and they use words to label that reality. These words or internal maps are the way each person thinks of events and people around them. But this map each of us has is not reality.

If two persons observe the same event, they may have two totally different recollections of the events and interpretations; this is because they have two different maps to draw from. NLP workers will often treat the memories as a metaphor, rather than an event itself.

8. All procedures should increase wholeness

This is based upon the prime directive that the unconscious mind works better as a whole, rather than fragmented parts. Therefore, everything that is done in NLP should promote wholeness, not fragmentation. Fragmentation creates internal and external conflict. You may find some NLP workers use this type of fragmentation to try to get results, but I do not. I believe that less conflict is better. People already have enough conflict in their lives, so anything that will reduce that and promote wholeness is optimal.

9. There is no failure, only feedback

This is an amazing presupposition. You cannot fail using NLP. There is only success and feedback for change.

When some people come to me for private sessions, they want to know exactly what I'm going to do, whether it is Hypnosis, Parts Integration, Anchoring, EFT or any other technique. My answer is, "I don't know. I don't know what is going to work for you for a particular problem or situation, but I'm going to use all of my skills and all of my care and all of my knowledge to make sure you get your results."

When you begin working with me, you will find that, first, I will listen very carefully to the words that you use, in order to have a deep understanding of YOUR map of the world and what you consider your limitations.

Nine times out of ten, what we do first will solve your issue; if that doesn't work; it doesn't mean we've failed. It just means we discovered a process that did not work for you on that particular issue. Consider the inventor Thomas Edison. It took him over one thousand trials to finally create the light bulb. When asked how he felt failing over 1,000 times he replied that he did not fail. He discovered 999 different ways not to make a light bulb.

Feedback is important for change. Albert Einstein said that the definition of insanity is to do the same thing over and over and expect different results. You must listen to feedback and accept it, and then change the behavior. So, if there is no failure, as long as you keep discovering and keep that healthy curiosity, you will find success.

10. The meaning of a communication is the response you get

In a typical conversation you may assume that each person is 50% responsible for the content and the understanding of what is being said. This means you say something and the other person is then half responsible for understanding your point of view in your communication.

In NLP, we take it a step further; a person is 100% responsible for communicating the meaning of what they are saying to others. This means you cannot ass-u-me anything. You should not gauge understanding by how well you think you explained your point to another, but both of us must rely on each other's responses. If we cannot repeat back exactly what we mean when we communicate with each other, we'll need to figure out a way to explain it better. Communication is the essence of solving problems in life.

Also, if you give up 50% of the responsibility for communication in a conversation, then you cannot change what you are doing. You will not get the proper feedback nor will you use it to alter your perception and response. You must be 100% responsible to assure that your message is being communicated clearly and then you can make adjustments. You must have the behavioral flexibility to make sure that you can make the necessary changes. An NLP Practitioner knows this and makes adjustments as they see it's needed to assure that you understand and are using correctly the techniques that you are learning. Here, there is absolutely no room for assumptions.

11. People have all the resources they need to succeed and to achieve their desired outcomes

This presupposition states that there are no un-resourceful people, only un-resourceful states. These states can be changed through NLP.

My role as a Master Practitioner is to help you get in touch with your inborn resources. This means that we have no limitations in our ability to learn. No matter who we are or what our circumstances are in life, we all have these resources ready to be unlocked and accessed.

There are, however, useful and un-useful strategies. Some strategies you are currently using do not get you the results you are seeking. In NLP you will be matched with the strategy that works for you. This may take some work, but there are strategies that NLP coaches can identify, which you may currently be using that are not working for you right now.

As mentioned earlier, labels can create a barrier to maximizing results. These create limited decision-making; but once these labels are released, a person can learn and grow. The good news is that beliefs work. The bad news is that beliefs work!

12. You are in charge of your mind and therefore your results

If you can structure your thinking to a positive flow of thoughts and outcomes, then success will occur. You are who you think you are; you are what you think. One of my mentors says, "You get what you focus on, so focus on what you want." There is an old saying that states: "What you focus on expands." The key here is to take control over what your internal representation of yourself is. You do have control over this.

Earlier we talked about who was "driving" you. You are! Many of us allow Mr. Babble to dictate our state of mind and internal representation. This is because we have allowed our minds to work on autopilot. You need to take your mind off of autopilot and allow your conscious mind to take back control of your bus, because it is in charge of thinking and setting the course and speed. A way to do this through NLP is if you have a negative thought, then you need to have positive thoughts supplant them. Over time, the supplanting positive thoughts will become automatic.

Where there is negative thinking, let there be contemplation to the contrary.

Patanjali – *Yoga Sutras*

Now that you know what the basic presuppositions of NLP are, you can better understand how NLP works and the guidelines under which both you and your NLP Practitioner will be working.

$\mathcal{P}$ERCEPTION IS

PROJECTION

✦ ✦ ✦

YOUR UNCONSCIOUS MIND HAS SO MUCH information to handle that it cannot deal with all of it. In a previous section you learned that your unconscious would delete, distort and generalize information. One of the ways that it does this is to project. This is what is meant by the phrase 'perception is projection'. When we have unresolved issues, we tend to project them onto others around us.

Consider people in your life right now and you may agree that you are projecting your thoughts and beliefs onto others. You may say that many of your friends and family are a lot like you. They like the same things and share ideas with you. These are not the people you are projecting on however.

It is those people you state that you have nothing in common with that you have the MOST in common with, unconsciously. This is because the emotions and thoughts you are having a hard time resolving in yourself, you may be projecting them.

This concept is very important in NLP, because it can really be a strong determining factor of how NLP impacts you and whether you can begin to see and resolve major life issues.

The information that is locked deep within us and we cannot resolve; we must project outwardly to people and events so that we can deal with them externally. However, this projection can really affect how we deal with people and the results we are going to get. It is our belief systems and filters that need to be strengthened and examined.

If we truly believe something to be true then it will become reality, or what may be considered 'our truth'. If we allow projections of issues to rule our decision-making process then these projections will become our reality. Remember, the unconscious will create exactly what we tell it to. It is always listening and waiting for instructions.

For instance, suppose you do not like someone because you think they are selfish. You may internally feel you are selfish and so you are seeing that part of yourself in them. You are projecting. It is an issue you need to deal with and resolve within yourself.

However, your belief that this person is selfish will create this reality. You will unconsciously create situations in this person that will make them act selfishly or you will filter what they do as being selfish. You believe they are selfish and therefore they become selfish. Because you have not resolved this issue within yourself, you then slide into living At Effect.

Let's look at how this projecting can affect groups of people. Suppose a new manager is placed in charge of a group of employees. He is told that they are lazy, not very bright and do not do enough work to reach production goals. The manager comes in with this idea and, lo and behold, in two weeks the employees are producing significantly less than the established production goals and sit around drinking coffee and talking a lot.

The next week a new manager is put in place. This manager is told that, this same group of employees was very motivated, over achievers, and energetic. In two weeks, this same group was considerably above production goals; and they were always working hard.

The manager's projection, based upon beliefs, impacted the way he interacted with the employees, and impacted the results as well. Beliefs and expectations are closely tied together. In NLP, your projections and beliefs are turned to more positive outcomes. If you believe you will succeed, you will! If you believe a person is good-natured and positive, you will bring that out in them.

Having the right NLP Practitioner is so important, as they must be skilled to know how to deal with situations like projection, and they must be aware of how they are projecting and what their beliefs are. The stronger their belief in their client the better the success will be.

Successful NLP Practitioners are aware of how their own beliefs can impact their clients. If they believe someone will not cooperate with them, or they feel their client will not succeed using NLP, then that will be the result.

If, on the other hand, they believe that the client in front of them is bright and motivated to succeed, then that will be the result. If they cannot get past a negative image of the client, then they are obligated to end the sessions or suggest they see another practitioner. A positive relationship is vital to success.

$\mathcal{S}$.M.A.R.T. GOALS

✦ ✦ ✦

AS A PERSON BEGINS TO USE NLP, they will want to develop goals on which to work. These are things that they want to accomplish, as this drives what NLP techniques you will use and the direction that the person wishes to go.

There is a difference between wants and needs. There are certain things that a person needs as a human. Psychologist Abraham Maslow developed a pyramid or hierarchy of needs. All of us find ourselves somewhere on this pyramid at different times in our lives.

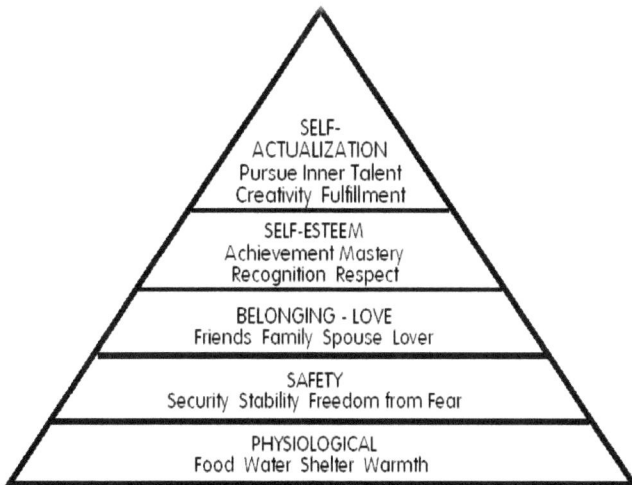

SELF-
ACTUALIZATION
Pursue Inner Talent
Creativity Fulfillment

SELF-ESTEEM
Achievement Mastery
Recognition Respect

BELONGING - LOVE
Friends Family Spouse Lover

SAFETY
Security Stability Freedom from Fear

PHYSIOLOGICAL
Food Water Shelter Warmth

Most of the time, we cannot navigate ourselves to the next level until we have satisfied the lower levels. We can get stuck on a particular level, which can create frustration and anxiety in our lives. NLP can help release barriers we may have on a particular level, so that we can transcend to the next.

For instance, suppose a person is having problems with relationships. This same person cannot keep a job and has been evicted from a number of places. This person cannot hope to begin working on the love/belonging level if they have not dealt with the lower levels of safety and physiological issues. An NLP worker can help the person assess where they are and work from that place, rather than ignoring the current circumstances to attempt to work on higher objectives. This is not to say these higher ideals should not be sought after; rather, the person must start where they are and make the journey one step at a time.

Each level of need has its own challenges; therefore, the person using the NLP strategies must be flexible. This is why using an NLP Coach can be so useful, as they can help you navigate your way through these levels, and help you when you might feel lost and in need of encouragement. The important thing to remember is that if you are struggling on lower levels of need, you need to take care of them first before trying work on more complicated needs.

Once you begin to meet your needs, you can begin to work on wants. Wants are usually more refined needs—a better job, a larger house, a life partner, etc. It is sometimes hard to separate needs from wants, but your needs have to be satisfied. You need to be able to make money at a job before you can hope to buy a large house.

As you begin to set goals that you want to accomplish, you should make sure that your goals are SMART:

S = Specific / Simple

M = Measurable / Meaningful to you

A = Achievable / As if now / All areas of your life

R = Realistic / Responsible (Ecological)

T = Time-specific / Toward what you want

Specific

The more specifically definable your goal is, the more likely it is that you will accomplish it. Do you recognize a target with a bull's-eye in the middle? There is just a small circle in the middle of much larger circles. This is the way you could think of the goals. You could focus on the essence of your goal and reduce it down to its essence.

If you can state your goal in a short phrase it's much better. Goals should be straightforward and emphasize what you want to happen.

Some of the things you may want to consider when creating a specific goal are the following:

How? How are you going to accomplish your goal?

Why? Why do you want to accomplish your goal?

What will the goal accomplish in your life? Does it fulfill a need or want?

What? What are you going to do to accomplish your goal? What tools and techniques will you use? What will you accomplish once you reach your goal?

The more clear and concise your goals are the more likely and the more rapidly you will reach them. It also helps set up the right NLP techniques for you to use.

Think about it like playing golf. The object is to get the ball in the hole. That's the goal of golf. In order to do this, you must hold and position your golf club in a certain way. Whichever way you point your club is the way the ball will travel. There are even traps and challenges along the way, but as long as you are sure of where your goal is, you can always make adjustments and eventually reach it. The more direct the route, the easier it is to find.

Simple

Remember that your unconscious is like that five-year-old genie. It's powerful enough to grant you every wish you have—provided you follow the rest of the criteria described here—, but you must keep the requests clear and simple.

What is it you want, really? How would you explain what you want to a five-year-old?

If you say you want to be successful, what does that even mean? To someone, success may mean not having to work on a job they don't like; to another, it may mean living in a certain city or neighborhood; to yet another, success may be having a loving family that enjoys spending time together.

The "nebulous" concept of *success* must be translated into a simple and concise representation. And so it is with *love, wealth, happiness, fulfillment,* and every other goal you have.

Measurable

The more measureable a goal is the easier it is to determine how close you are to attaining your goal. Measuring a goal allows you to manage it. Your goal statement is a measure of what you want to accomplish. If you accomplish your goal, then it is a clear measure of success. You can also have some short-term goals within your larger goal. These can be markers along the way.

Imagine you want a specific type of job. The first measure is looking online and finding the jobs that match your skills. Then, your next measure is getting your resume out to these companies. Then, the next measure is receiving a call for an interview, or for a second interview; and your final and largest goal is that you have landed the job that you wanted.

You can create a list of these smaller goals, and NLP will help you break down any barriers along the way.

The statement 'I want a job' may not be measureable. A statement of "I want a job that pays $100,000 a year and has three weeks of paid vacation with a great healthcare plan and bonuses" is much more measureable. It is specific, and it is also something that you can measure for success. The more specific the criteria are towards achieving your goal (for example, paid vacations and a certain salary level), the more it will ensure that you are going after the specific goal, with specific details that you hope to accomplish.

Meaningful to You

Remember that one of the prime directives is that your unconscious mind takes everything personally. Your goals should give YOU pleasure and fulfillment. Even if you're working for others, some part of that achievement must be meaningful to you.

Meaningful to you also means tangible. I always laugh to myself when I hear the classical answer from the Miss Universe contestants as to their goals when they say, "World Peace."

Your unconscious mind doesn't know what "world peace" means. It's a foreign concept, far too removed from it to be understood. If you DO, consciously, want to work on "world peace," you must translate that ethereal phrase into something that is Meaningful to you, such as "My community gets along, and neighbors share their resources," or something like this.

As If Now

When you set your goals, remember that your unconscious mind has no experience of time tenses, other than the present. There is no practical concept for the past or the future. When you remember something from the past, such as a traumatic event, what you're actually doing is bringing those memories into the present and reliving them in the here and now. That's why they hurt. If they were in the past (meaning they're over and done with), you would not hurt when you remember them.

But don't believe me. Experience this yourself.

Do you have a memory of a "less than positive" experience from the past that, when you remember it, no longer bothers you? That is something that is in your practical past—it's done.

Now, if you were to remember an experience that still bothers you, you may notice that you're actually bringing the memory into the present and reliving it. **Stop it!**

The best thing about the past is that it's over.

We'll talk more about how to let go of things from the past and how to leave them there, but the point I'm making here is that you can only experience the present. So, when you write your goals, you must write them as if they are happening right now.

Think about it. If you write, "I will make $1,000,000" next week the instructions to your unconscious is "I will make $1,000,000" and next month your unconscious will continue with "I will make $1,000,000", and the year after that your unconscious is thinking "I will make $1,000,000" because the fulfillment of the goal is always in the future. Think about the beam of light on the headlights of a car; no matter how fast the car goes it will never reach the headlight beam because it's always out in front.

Write your goals in the present tense, "as if now" you have your goal. Your unconscious mind understands this practically.

Achievable

Do not set yourself up for failure. It is appropriate and desirable that you push yourself beyond your normal expectations, but you have to make sure you can actually achieve the goal you set for yourself. Setting up unrealistic goals not only makes them impossible to attain but it also can damage your confidence for setting and accomplishing future goals.

Setting achievable goals also helps motivate your unconscious mind to accomplish them; you can come up with ways to make your dreams a reality. You will then develop your positive attitude and outlook, because you know that the goals are right within your reach. This positive outlook helps you see opportunities clearly when they present themselves to you. Your unconscious mind can help direct you because you will be listening to your intuition and following your own inner guidance. This communication is improved by using NLP techniques consistently and effectively.

If you set unachievable goals, you will not be very motivated. You will listen more closely to the voice of Mr. Babble than you will to your unconscious mind. You will begin to develop an attitude of failure, which, in effect, will program your unconscious mind to do exactly that—fail.

Suppose you are just over five feet tall but you want to be an Air Force pilot. The height requirement for the United States Air Force pilots is 64"-77" (5'4"-6'-5") standing; sitting it is 33"-40" (2'9"-3'4"). Therefore, unless you are under 18 years old and still expecting a growth spurt, the goal of becoming a pilot is not achievable. However, if you want to be a commercial airline or freight pilot, this may be more achievable, as there are different height requirements for obtaining a commercial pilot's license. If it is just the Air Force you are interested in, you can still look for other careers within the USAF that do not have the height restrictions of combat pilots.

The more achievable a goal is the more likely it is that you will work hard to attain it. If you know that losing 40lbs in a month is not achievable, then the likelihood of losing any weight will be slim (pun intended). However, if you are looking to lose one to two pounds a week, this type of goal is much more achievable.

All Areas of Your Life

You are a multifaceted and multitalented human being. As such, you have many areas that comprise your life. In the upcoming section "Include All Areas of Your Life" we go into exquisite detail about this very topic.

For now, let's just say that, in order to live a balanced and fulfilled life, our goals and our growth must take place in all of these areas.

Have you ever known someone who is great at making money, but their personal relationships are in the dumps? Do you know of people who are extremely religious, but their health leaves much to be desired? They may excel in one area, but neglect other areas of their lives.

Truly successful and satisfied people have goals for all areas of their lives. I did mention earlier that your goal must be specific. So, when you write your goals, write a goal that is specific to that area of your life, and be sure to write goals for each area.

Realistic

Being realistic is similar to assuring yourself that your goal is achievable. This indicates whether a goal is actually doable by you. You might have an achievable goal but it may not be doable by you. This is the difference between possible and probable. It is possible to do many different things in life, but that does not mean that they are all probable to occur. It is possible to win the lottery. Every ticket has the same chance of winning on any given day.

However, it's not probable that you will win the lottery. Setting unrealistic goals can be as bad as setting unachievable goals.

Realistically, you could still motivate and push yourself to reach for your dreams, but 'to thine own self be true', wrote The Bard. And, Shakespeare must have known something about the mind mechanics of success because his plays were filled with the philosophy behind life. In the real world, if you are not honest with yourself, the consequences can be fatal.

For instance, suppose you want to become a doctor. It is definitely something that is achievable. Many people become doctors, but suppose you are not very good in math and science. You might be able to get through medical school, but is it even realistic? How much math is involved with medical school? WOW, then you will struggle a lot and may not achieve your goal, because you may have constant 'let's give up' thoughts, or you just may not be able to pass the math classes.

There are ways you can make a goal more realistic. Maybe you can get extra tutoring in math or go into a different career field within the medical field that does not require as much math. Psychiatrists require more math than psychologists. LPN's require less math than RN's.

Make a plan on how to make the goal more realistic. Then take into consideration where you are at this moment in your life. That's becoming aware of your "here-and-now" reality.

It is difficult for some to imagine buying a $1,000,000 home if they are in a job making $43,000 a year. So you can either change the value of the home you are looking for or push yourself towards getting a better-paying job. Either of these solutions will make the goal more realistic.

You might still set the bar high enough to make sure you are satisfied with your achievement. If the goal is too high and you fail you will not feel very successful, however.

If, on the other hand, you are aiming your skills too low, even if you achieve the goal, you may not feel very satisfied with the experience. You also may not feel that you have attained any further capabilities, or that you are even successful. Consider the bull's-eye. If you can shoot an arrow fairly well, and you are only standing two feet from the target, you might easily get the bull's-eye. But it won't be very satisfying to you.

On the other hand, if you stand across a field, your goal is more achievable and it will stretch your skills somewhat, and it is still realistic for most people. However, if you blindfold yourself, the goal can still be achievable, but not very realistic.

Using NLP techniques can open up new possibilities for you. What you may have thought was unachievable or unrealistic can become possible. Many times it is your own fears and doubts that can obscure goals or even make them unachievable. Once you remove fears, goals become very achievable. When you begin to achieve things that you once thought impossible, your confidence will increase simultaneously. It opens up far greater possibilities for you. You are building on your successes, and you're taking your masterpiece to the next level of achievement.

Responsible (Ecological)

We talked about Ecology before. This means that in setting your goals, you take into consideration your own wellbeing, the wellbeing of all those involved, the wellbeing of your community, and the wellbeing of the world.

Deep in your unconscious mind, there is a part that is looking out for ecology. If your goal is to make a million dollars, but you have to sell inferior products to people, you're much less likely to achieve that, because you're violating your Ecological check.

You may say, "But there are people out there who are doing things that are not ecological." True. But how truly successful are they in the long run? Sooner or later, they will be found out and brought to justice, and they never really enjoyed success and satisfaction, anyway.

Time-Specific

Setting the right timeframe is very important in achieving goals. Remember the example of losing 40 pounds in one month. This timeframe is neither attainable nor realistic, and this is because of the timeframe. People lose forty pounds all the time. They do it over a reasonable amount of time.

It is important to set a time in your goal making. This helps keep you on track and have an arrival time. When you book a flight to a destination, you usually look at when the plane lands. If you did not see an arrival time, this might make you a little nervous. Will the plane just be flying around aimlessly? Are there other destinations along the way? Will the pilot land the plane for a while to take a nap? Knowing when you are going to arrive at a destination is important.

Setting a time for you to achieve your goal becomes a promise you make to yourself that you will reach it. If you tell someone that you will meet him or her at 2:00 tomorrow, then you are making a promise to him or her. When 2:00 rolls around, the expectation is that you will meet each other at the agreed upon location. Setting a time for a goal is similar. You are saying that on a certain date, and maybe even a specific time, you will arrive at your goal.

If you do not set a time for your goal, then this can be too vague. Consider the example above. If you told your friend that you would meet them sometime this week, then they would not have an expectation that they would ever see you, except by accident.

Some time ago, I heard the story of Mae Laborde, a 100-year-old actress (born May 13, 1909) who did a series of commercials for the Fox Network and the FX channel. The most astonishing fact about Mae's story is that she started in the acting business at the age of 93! In an interview, she said that she "always wanted to do this" (acting).

She had a goal to become an actress—perhaps it was even her passion—, but she never made her goal time-specific. It is imperative that your goal be specific as to the time, otherwise you may get the achievement of your goal, but much later than you imagine. What if you had a goal to meet the love of your life? You go through your entire life without meeting that special someone.

Then, on your deathbed, you finally see in the eyes of your nurse that spark you were always looking for. "Your wish is my command." It's been granted, but a bit too late to enjoy fully.

Without setting a time on your goal there will be no urgency to achieve it. It would mean you could start any time and arrive anytime. The likelihood of you arriving at your goal would be by pure chance alone.

Like other aspects of goal setting, setting a time must be realistic and achievable. If you give yourself too much time, you may become bored and not be too motivated. Suppose you want to go back to school. If you say in the next 5 years you might want to go back to school, you might not be motivated to do what it takes to get there. If on the other hand the time is too short, such as "next month I want to be back in college," this may not be realistic or achievable, as you may need to take some tests, get your transcripts, write some essays, etc.

Toward What You Want

There are two basic types of motivation that drive everything we do: Pain and Pleasure. We seek to avoid pain and to gain pleasure. In NLP, these are known as Propulsion Systems.

If you've ever seen a rocket launch to the Moon, it is an impressive sight to behold. After the countdown reaches zero, the rumble of the solid rocket boosters fills the air, and an impressive 7.8 million pounds of thrust overcomes gravity's pull, launching the spacecraft to about 18,000 miles per hour. The initial force to escape Earth's gravity is immense. But that's not all.

After the spacecraft leaves the Earth's atmosphere, it takes very little to maintain speed. After a while, as the spacecraft comes closer to the Moon, our Satellite's gravitational force actually pulls the spacecraft toward it.

It's the same thing with our goals. You can have two foci in any particular goal. If the area of your life you're working on is relationships, you can have an overall goal to meet the person that will be your partner for life.

Within that goal, it is essential to know *why* you want that relationship. Is it to enjoy life and share your gifts and talents with another person, or is it so you won't be lonely?

Do you notice the difference?

In the first *reason*, you're moving towards something you want (sharing of yourself with another human being), while in the other *reason* your focus is away from what you don't want (to be lonely).

At first, this may take some introspection and honesty on your part. You can't just say, "Yes, I want to share my life with another person" only because you just read that. Again, "To thine own self be true." What is the *real* reason that YOU want to have that relationship?

It's important to know, because the focus of your work will be different in each case. Imagine if the space shuttle crew would simply wait for the Moon's gravitational pull to do its thing. Nothing would ever happen.

An NLP Practitioner can help you define your Toward and Away From motivators. The best strategy is to use a combination of both. First, the Away From motivation needs to be strong enough to overcome inertia—the cost of doing nothing. Then, once you're far away from the thing that got you moving in the first place, you engage the Toward motivation to pull you to your optimal life, Your Masterpiece.

On the next page is a worksheet that we use in my Goals Seminars and I provide to my private clients, which serves as a reminder of, and a primer for the elements of a well-formed goal.

Using the SMART method, while utilizing NLP techniques, can move mountains for you. You will be amazed how easily you can achieve the goals you may have been trying to achieve your entire life without success.

Write goals for each area of your life, and use the SMART Goal Worksheet on the next page so you're sure to include all these factors.

S.M.A.R.T. GOALS

S Specific
Simple

M Measurable
Meaningful to you

A As if now
Achievable
All areas of your life

R Realistic
Responsible/Ecological

T Time-specific
Toward what you want

Decide Who You Want To Be

It is time to start envisioning Your Masterpiece. All the masters have a vision of what the finished product will look like.

I dream my painting, and then I paint my dream

Vincent Van Gogh

But before you go on to create Your Masterpiece, you need to set a starting point. And the starting point for creating your life is to take full responsibility for where you are right now in your life.

As I mentioned in the beginning of the book, you do this by being "At Cause" for everything in your life, not "At Effect."

Consider where you are in life. There is a road that is behind you—it contains the good and the bad. There were conscious choices and unconscious ones, but all of them led you to where you are at this very moment. No one else brought you to where you are—you did it all yourself. (Including the decision to buy this book.) Congratulate yourself!

As you begin to reconstruct your life, it is time to make a conscious choice. You must make the choice to walk on the At Cause side of life. Two roads are before you at this crossroads in your life: Life 'At Cause' and Life 'At Effect'. It is time to take the At Cause way. In the future, when you look back to now, you will see how you ended up where you did, just like you can right now.

Cause = Results

Effect = Reasons

When you live your life At Cause, you will have results. These are the results of your labor and conscious choices. On the other hand, if you live life At Effect, all you can expect are reasons. These are the reasons why you are not seeing results in your life. This is the blame game the people who live At Effect in life love.

If you live At Effect in life, you will not be alone. As you think of reasons, there will always be those near you to support those reasons. They will say "You poor thing." Or, "You never had a chance in life" or "If you did not have such bad luck you would have no luck at all." The nature of "support" groups is that they can support all the failure reasons why you have not succeeded. You will never have to look far for the sympathy of others that support your living 'At Effect' lifestyle.

This is not to say that all the 'not so good things' that happen in life are our fault or that we consciously chose them. What I am saying is that conscious and unconscious choices (automatic responses) lead us down our own life path.

The beauty of Neuro-Linguistic Programming is that it helps people transition from reasons to results—from effects to causes. Once you have decided to live on the 'At Cause' side of the equation, you will begin to learn from life. Once you get to this stage of learning, you will have unlocked the key to making the bright future of your own creation. You will be on your way to Making Your Life Your Masterpiece.

HAPPINESS FROM WITHIN

✦ ✦ ✦

I BELIEVE IT WAS GALILEO WHO SAID "You cannot teach a man anything; you can only help him to find it within himself." And, so it goes with happiness. You have within you everything you need to be happy. It's just a matter of finding the right combination of thoughts, attitudes and actions... that's right, ACTIONS! All the great and illuminated thinkers have said that you have to BE before you can DO, in order that you can HAVE.

"The game of life is a game of boomerangs. Our thoughts, deeds and words return to us sooner or later with astounding accuracy."

-Florence Scovel Shinn, writer, artist and teacher (1871-1940)

Many people look for happiness externally. They look for it in their careers or their partners and even in their children. They buy many material things with the belief that if they just buy that bigger car or larger house that they would be happy. They buy into the belief that money can make you happy or that if they marry the right girl or guy then they will live the fairy tale life, and live happily ever after.

Even if some of these things may give a person some moments of happiness, they are just that: momentary. The capacity for any car or material object to make us happy in the long term is itself a fairytale.

The truth of the matter is that only true happiness can be found within. Don't take my word for it; consider the words of wisdom about happiness from some of the greatest minds of our time and throughout history:

Democritus, (460BC-370BC)

Happiness resides not in possessions and not in gold, the feeling of happiness dwells in the soul.

Aristotle

To live happily is an inward power of the soul.

Sharon Salzberg

It doesn't matter how long we may have been stuck in a sense of our limitations. If we go into a darkened room and turn on the light, it doesn't matter if the room has been dark for a day, a week, or ten thousand years—we turn on the light and it is illuminated. Once we control our capacity for love and happiness, the light has been turned on.

John Templeton

Happiness comes from spiritual wealth, not material wealth... Happiness comes from giving, not getting. If we try hard to bring happiness to others, we cannot stop it from coming to us also. To get joy, we must give it, and to keep joy, we must scatter it.

Ursula K. LeGuin

I certainly wasn't happy. Happiness has to do with reason, and only reason earns it. What I was given was the thing you can't earn, and can't keep, and often don't even recognize at the time; I mean joy.

Mary Baker Eddy

Happiness is spiritual, born of Truth and Love. It is unselfish; therefore it cannot exist alone, but requires all mankind to share it.

Unknown

Take care of yourself. Good health is everyone's major source of wealth. Without it, happiness is almost impossible.

Martha Washington

The greater part of our happiness or misery depends on our dispositions, and not on our circumstances. We carry the seeds of the one or the other about with us in our minds wherever we go.

Lord Byron

All who would win joy, must share it; happiness was born a twin.

Anonymous

Happiness is not having what you want, but wanting what you have.

Ludwig Wittgenstein

The world of those who are happy is different from the world of those who are not.

Unknown

The really happy person is one who can enjoy the scenery when on a detour.

Diogenes Laertius, Zeno

One ought to seek out virtue for its own sake, without being influenced by fear or hope, or by any external influence. Moreover, that in that does happiness consist.

Victor Hugo

The supreme happiness in life is the conviction that we are loved—loved for ourselves, or rather, loved in spite of ourselves.

Picasso

Everything exists in limited quantity—especially happiness.

Margaret Lee Runbeck

Happiness is not a station you arrive at, but a manner of traveling.

John B. Sheerin

Happiness is not in our circumstance but in ourselves.
It is not something we see, like a rainbow, or feel, like the heat of a fire. Happiness is something we are.

Allan K. Chalmers

The Grand essentials of happiness are: something to do, something to love, and something to hope for.

Anonymous

Happiness is enhanced by others but does not depend upon others.

Happiness, then, is within reach for all of us. In her bestselling book *Happy for No Reason*, Marci Shimoff presents practical tips on how to raise your level of happiness every day. Marci shares a new paradigm of happiness. Her main message is that everything you need to be happier is inside of you.

So, I wonder if you're ready to put into practice Marci's advice, starting with the title of her book. Be happy for no reason at all.

$\mathcal{I}$NCLUDE ALL AREAS OF YOUR LIFE

✦ ✦ ✦

PEOPLE ARE MULTIFACETED INDIVIDUALS. They have many different aspects that make them who they are. For instance consider the many roles I play in life:

I am a son. I call my dad and visit him whenever I can, and I visit my mom as often as I can. This is one of the roles that define who I am and also defines what I do.

I am father. I provide love, support, and discipline to my children. This defines the actions I take, and how I identify myself through those actions.

I indentify myself as a brother. I provide support and a role to my siblings. This role, like other roles in my life, has evolved over time, even though the title or label that identifies this role has remained the same. You may be experiencing this label identity in a similar way.

I am a NLP Trainer, Coach, Business Owner, community leader, President of the Santa Ana Lions Club, and the President of my Toastmasters Club. Each of these roles identifies things I do. They are comprised of attitudes, actions and behaviors. When someone asks who a person is, they will usually reply with the job that they do; but as you can see, who you are encompasses many different roles, responsibilities and expectations.

In NLP there are many different areas that are focused upon. It is the whole person that is important, not just one or two small parts. If you concentrate on just one part, you may fail to affect the entire person. This can lead to discontentment and unhappiness. You may have seen these types of people that seem to have everything that a person could want but they still seem unhappy. This is because there are some areas of their life that have been missed or that are out of balance with the rest.

Patricia, one of my clients, was a very successful woman, and a highly sought-after community leader. She was in charge of this, and president of that, and was always giving of herself and her talents. She was a great Mother and a model wife. She was a great friend to many, and was always there for anyone who needed her. Still, she didn't feel fulfilled.

As we explored her emptiness, I asked her, "When was the last time you did something purely and absolutely for yourself?" She drew a blank. She thought, searched and dug deep in her memory for an answer. She could not remember the last time she did something that was only for her.

You can guess what her assignment was.

Consider a woman who wants a great career position. She works hard on just that one aspect—suppose it is in advertising. She works on getting into college. She goes to the college of her choice, and is in the program that she has chosen. Things look great. She spends many hours studying and graduates at the head of her class.

Because she has done so well the firm that she really wants to get into hires her. She starts at the lowest level and by working extra hours and weekends she moves up the corporate ladder. She is now middle-aged and on top of her game. She has an expensive car, the house she always dreamed of, and plenty of cash in the bank.

When she goes home at night and is settling down, she feels empty. She has everything that she could have possibly hoped for in a career, but that is really all she has. She has worked so many hours and given her life to that pursuit that she now realizes that she is coming home to an empty home every night. There is no one to greet her and the extra rooms, while decorated with all of the most elegant fashions by big-name designers, cannot make up for the feeling of the rooms not having children in them. She is alone and unhappy.

She had a couple of love affairs, but these were short-lived because of the amount of time and effort that she put into her career. She only realized too late that there were other roles in her life that she neglected and which, in the end, were connected to true happiness. She has all the money in the world but she could not buy a family or buy back the time she was missing.

She had not talked to her sister in years, and was not even sure what she was up to or how old her niece and nephew were. Her parents got a card from the different places she visited during the holidays, usually alone.

NLP can really make a huge impact in people's lives. It will give you exactly what you are asking for, but before you begin you need to make an inventory of exactly what you want. It's important to be clear about your life, your desires and your needs. A well-versed NLP Practitioner can help you look at your life as a whole rather than a collection of disjointed pieces.

Sometimes we can get caught up in just one aspect. This is easy to do, since most of the time we prioritize our needs and goals and then go through this list as we begin accomplishing. It is important to check in to make sure you are improving your entire life, and not just focusing on those one or two aspects. Remember, with NLP you will get exactly what you ask for. Your unconscious mind is not very good at interpreting accurately what we want, and may not fill in any gaps we miss. It just does what we tell it to do. The conscious mind is driving the bus remember?

My friend, Bart Baggett, in his book *Success Secrets of the Rich and Happy* (which I had the pleasure of translating into Spanish a few years back), presents a beautiful illustration of this balance of the different aspects of your life.

He came up with it as he was meditating on some of the basic principles of the mind that we've mentioned here (he's trained in NLP), and he combined it with Steven Covey's concept of categorizing your time in quadrants to stay away from urgency and to focus in what is really important.

He calls it your "Life Board," which gives you a visual representation of your life in balance. Let me illustrate:

Take a pencil and a piece of paper and get involved in the creation of a visual diagram for your life. Draw a big circle and divide it in four quadrants. Mark each of them as in the next diagram:

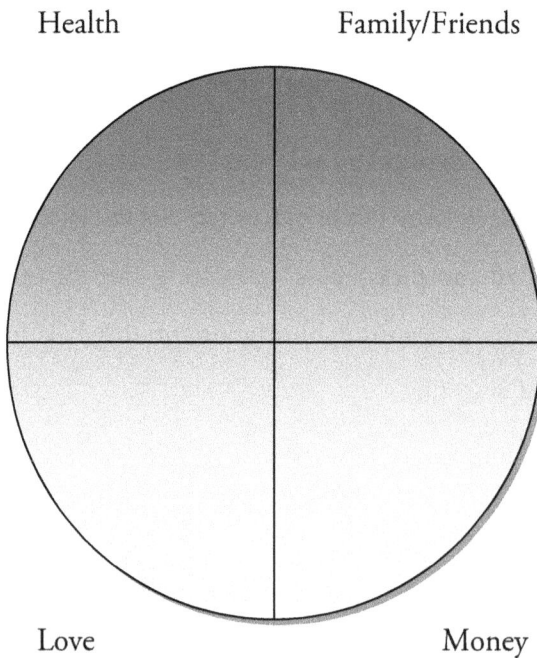

Health   Family/Friends

Love   Money

In each quadrant, write the three most important things going on in your life that you're dealing with in each category. For instance, if you have a disease, write that disease in the Health category. If you are divorced, write the name of your spouse in the Love category. If you believe your father is a moron, write his name in the Family/Friends category. If you struggle to pay your bills every month, write *bills* in the Money quadrant. By the way, when you do your own Life Board, do not limit yourself to just four categories. Some people have added their own categories, such as 'Spiritual/Religion' or 'Hobbies/Creativity', etc. But in order to simplify the illustration, only use four quadrants for the demonstration.

Bart talks about the concepts of Story versus Drama. Your story is your interpretation of the events going on in your life, plain and simple. Drama, on the other hand, is all those things that we add subconsciously to spice up our stories.

If a cop pulls you over for not making a full stop at a stop sign, you can recount what happened in a straightforward manner, and that is your story. Perhaps he was mean or stern; maybe he gave you a lecture on the perils of the "California Roll" and that was that.

If you start telling of how he was just hiding behind a blind corner waiting for YOU to blow the stop sign, and how he stopped YOU because of this or that, and how you argued for 45 minutes with him about the laws of physics and inertia, and why it takes more time and energy to start motion on a vehicle from a full stop and you were only trying to be kinder to the planet by not making a complete stop, and he STILL gave you a ticket, that is your drama.

The first step is your actual stories. What is going on in your life right now regarding unplanned health issues? Write any event you might be dealing with: depression, cancer, flu, broken leg, a friend's health problem, etc. What is going on right now in your love life? Make a list. Do the same with money and with family.

Now, when you are done writing some of your favorite stories, draw an inner circle and an outer circle. Mark the inner circle as 'Intentional Emotion' and the outer circle 'Outer Drama'.

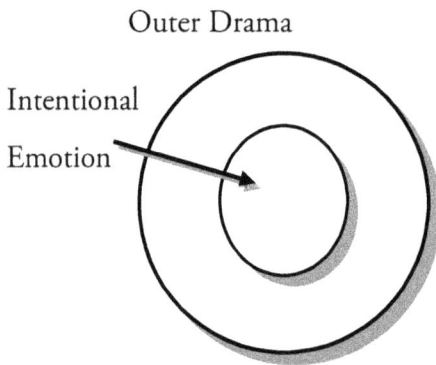

Outer Drama

Intentional
Emotion

Look at your stories and notice which ones are created by the 'world' and which ones were created by you because they bring you pleasure and realization.

I asked you to mark the outer circle with *Outer Drama*. This is the 'default' zone in which most of the events in your life happen, if you do not have fixed intentions.

Now, in your mind, place that disc on the floor and make it bigger, about six feet in diameter. Picture yourself standing in the center of that inner circle. Look around. Are the areas balanced? Are there more events in your love life than in your health area? Are you spending too much time in the money/career section and ignoring your love life? Once you have a clear picture of standing in the center of the disc, close your eyes. Imagine using your sense of inner balance in order to balance yourself and remain centered.

Well, that's pretty easy if the board is on the floor in the middle of your living room. So, let's add an element of risk to the game.

Imagine you are standing on your Life Board but now the board is on a rubber ball that is three feet in diameter. Now, keep the balance. Focus. Sure, it's easy to maintain your balance, as long as nobody jumps into your 'love' area and you suffer an emotional crisis. The "drama weight" of that person takes the focus off of the remaining quadrants.

When you live your life on purpose, when you're in charge of the stories and the drama you allow (or not allow) in your life, your Life Board remains in balance and you decide what your focus will be.

For a while, now, I have decided that if someone or something is not serving to keep the balance and harmony in my life, they don't get to play, work or spend much time with me.

So, let's work on YOUR Life Board. What are the different areas of your life? You can use these suggestions, and add or delete as you like. After all, it's YOUR LIFE.

Career

Love

Family

Money

Entertainment

Causes you are interested in

Hobbies/ Recreational activities

The list can go on, and it is different for everyone. It is one of the things that make us unique. Sometimes we may get caught up with external programming. These are the messages from our parents and society about what is important and what roles we should play. Those may fall into the category of "drama." Sometimes this works out for us and sometimes it doesn't. It is what is within you that are important. If you tell your unconscious mind that the main thing you want is a happy, well-balanced life, then your unconscious mind will oblige. But you have to be specific as to what you mean. Remember the KISS principle: Keep It Sweet and Simple.

Picture yourself on the disc of your Life Board; you're standing there, watching the different areas of your life. You're in balance. Everything is OK.

Then, something happens and suddenly, you lost $50,000 in the Stock Market. Then, a car hits your dog. Or your mother ends up in the hospital. So, how do you keep the balance? If you have created emotional, physical and even financial savings in each quadrant... then there is no problem. You can leave the center of the disc, deal with the emergency, and then return to the center. Your weight will not unbalance the disc if you have invested time in each quadrant before the crisis arrives.

What most people do is this: They spend their time in the outer circle running from quadrant to quadrant like a mouse in a wheel, running from one side to the other, dealing with emergency after emergency. This is what Steven Covey calls living in 'urgency'.

Focus on health, relationships, career, spirit, family and money. If you are unfocused too much, you will fall out of your Life Board. Then you will stand up again, only to fall down again at the next bluff in the way. Life can turn out to be too frustrating if you cannot keep your balance.

And the way you keep yourself balanced is very, very simple: Make good decisions. Each moment of every day, you have the choice to decide which thoughts you focus on. Every day invest time to ask yourself: *What can I do to create intentional emotion in each of these quadrants? How can I make an emotional deposit in my relationships, my family and friends?*

Picture yourself driving tomorrow. Somebody cuts you off and almost crashes into you. You have the choice about what you allow to dwell in your mind, and what you are going to do next. This is what we call a decision. Choose happiness. Keep your balance. It sounds so simple. It is simple.

WHAT STOPS YOU FROM BEING THERE NOW?

✦ ✦ ✦

AS YOU BEGIN CREATING YOUR LIFE as Your Masterpiece through NLP, you will look closely at where you are in your life right now. This includes the good and the bad, as well as all of what makes up who we are. There are a few things that must be dealt with first in order for us to move toward creating our life as the masterpiece we have always wanted.

Consider Lance Armstrong for a moment. Controversies aside, he is the multi-time winner of the Tour de France (So much so, that they should consider changing the name of the event to 'Tour de Lance'). If you have ever watched the race, you will notice something about how Lance and all the competitors are dressed. They are wearing the lightest and the most aerodynamic clothes possible. Even their bikes are made from Titanium alloys that make them super light.

This is because Lance Armstrong knows that in order to cross that finish line first they must be as strong and light as possible. Having a heavy bike or one full of extra baggage would only slow them down, and eventually they would stop before they ever reached the finish line.

We carry some of this heavy baggage around every day, and it is what slows us down and prevents us from reaching the finish line.

Lance Armstrong also has an interesting story. He had cancer that threatened his life. He overcame it and came back stronger and faster than ever. If he carried that baggage of cancer with him, he would never have qualified to even get into the race, let alone win it year after year.

He decided to leave that baggage behind. All the worry, anxiety, sickness, depression and fear were left behind when his cancer went into remission. Lance was free; his mind and body were light and he moved like a bullet train through the small mountain villages in France. Nothing held him back. He became a hero and never let some rather tough life circumstances keep him from reaching his goal—again and again. The world was so amazed that they had Lance tested for performance-enhancing drugs over and over again. Even this did not slow him down. He was already a winner in his mind and his body. Even recovering from cancer moved the way it was directed. Lance won the Tour de France in his mind before he ever put his bike at the starting line.

CLEAR NEGATIVITY FROM THE PAST

So, part of what is holding us in the place where we are stuck is what lies behind us. Imagine for a moment walking down a road in the cool evening. Ahead you see bright lights, and you can even hear music. This is your bright and exciting future ahead of you. You can see the road you have chosen and you see that it leads straight to your destination. It is a clear and straight path. You feel excited and motivated about the possibilities that await you. You take a step forward and find that you cannot move. YOU'RE STUCK!

You look back and realize that there is a large chain around your ankle and it is connected to something behind you. You see a huge pile of old baggage with the large chain wrapped around all of it. It is too heavy to move. This is your past and the baggage you have chosen to bring with you on your life journey. It is a choice to bring this baggage with you, but you will find that it is almost impossible to move forward with it chained to you.

The great thing about baggage from the past is that you have the key to unlock that chain and leave it all behind. NLP offers great ways to do this. Once you release and dissolve that chain, you can leave the baggage where it belongs—in the past. This restraint is what keeps us stuck, because it promotes negative thoughts and behavior. It is what keeps Mr. Babble babbling in our heads. It is what plays on our fears and doubts. Past negativity will reproduce into present and future negativity.

The first step in the process of releasing the baggage is recognizing and accepting that it is there. You can look through the baggage and see the bad experiences, and accept them as part of who you are; but know that they do not define you. They were learning experiences, but you are not keeping your spelling books from first grade are you? You learn the lessons, you integrate them into your life and then you let them go. Sometimes letting go can be difficult and emotional, and that is why working with an NLP Practitioner is so important.

MAKE A LIST OF ALL THE INCOMPLETE THINGS IN YOUR LIFE

There are always two sides to a coin. In this case, I have talked about releasing the past and the negative thoughts associated with it. On the flip side is to look for gaps in our lives. What things in our life have we started and put off, that we have never completed? Are there areas in your life that you would like to pursue, but never had the courage to?

All the things that are incomplete in your life are dragging you down. If you consider that when we do something we put our energy into it until it is completed, imagine all the energy that is escaping when you have incomplete things in your life. Don't believe me? Look at your experience.

When you're working on a project, whatever it may be, how do you feel when it is finished? Don't you feel a sense of relief? (Especially if it took you a long time to complete it) It's as if you ended a chapter of your life; and, if you have a list of things to do, don't you feel like you have more energy as you start checking things off?

When you have incomplete things in your life, they are sapping your energy. So, if you want to have more energy to create your masterpiece, complete those unfinished things in your life.

You can make a list of these incomplete things with your NLP Practitioner. These are areas and goals you can work on. Recently, there was a movie called "The Bucket List" (2007) with Jack Nicholson and Morgan Freeman. The premise of the movie is that two people were dying and there was a list of things that they always wanted to do, and they began a journey to complete them. None of us really knows when our time is up, so never put off until tomorrow what you can do today.

WHAT PREVENTS YOU FROM LIVING THE LIFE THAT YOU WANT NOW?

The great thing is that you have the power to make your life anything you want it to be. The bad news is that you have the power to make your life anything you want it to be. The greatest barrier you will encounter in attempting to achieve your goals is not some external force. It is the person staring back at you in the mirror every morning.

This is not about pointing fingers, playing the blame game or you feeling guilty. Those are negative emotions and serve no positive purpose. You have the ability and the choice to change your life. There are many external forces that may have made you believe you do not have the power, and on top of that you have Mr. Babble trying to convince you that you will fail; but the truth is that you have the power to succeed. NLP helps you remove these barriers and helps send the right messages to your unconscious. The more dedicated and consistent you are with the process, the more likely it is that you will see results.

IS THERE A PART OF YOU THAT DOES NOT WANT THIS TO HAPPEN?

Most of us do not like change. We are more comfortable in situations in which we are accustomed. We like to know what to expect, even if it is not the results we are looking for. A person can stay working as a fry cook for years. They would not mind being a manager and may have even dreamed of doing it. However, they remain the fry cook because they are afraid of change. They are afraid of taking a risk, which is involved with change.

So there is a part of us that will resist change. This is natural, as it is an inborn instinct. An animal will not usually go into a new part of the forest. They will stay close to where they live. In a different part of the forest there are untold dangers. This change could be unsafe for the animal. We are the same way; change can make us feel unsafe. Whether or not the risk is high, we may feel anxious or even self-sabotage our own efforts. It is this fear that has us working against ourselves.

Remember that one of the prime directives of the unconscious mind is to preserve the body. If what you have been doing all these years is working for you, your unconscious mind will continue to do that, because so far it has worked... you're alive.

Doing something new or different may or may not keep you safe, so this is why our unconscious mind resists change.

Here are some words of wisdom about change and its importance to inspire you and give your unconscious some food for thought. Once we use NLP, we can help ourselves get out of our own way and allow change to occur.

If you don't like something change it; if you can't change it,
change the way you think about it.

~Mary Engelbreit

All changes, even the most longed for, have their melancholy; for what we leave behind us is a part of ourselves; we must die to one life before

we can enter another.

~Anatole France

When we are no longer able to change a situation, we are challenged to change ourselves.

~Victor Frankl

The man who looks for security, even in the mind, is like a man who would chop off his limbs in order to have artificial ones which will give him no pain or trouble.

~Henry Miller

When you are through changing, you are through.

~Bruce Barton

They must often change, who would be constant in happiness or wisdom.

~Confucius

Life is its own journey, presupposes its own change and movement, and one tries to arrest them at one's eternal peril.

~Laurens van der Post

Growth is the only evidence of life.

~John Henry Newman, Apologia pro vita sua, 1864

The circumstances of the world are so variable that an irrevocable purpose or opinion is almost synonymous with a foolish one.

~William H. Seward

Stubbornness does have its helpful features. You always know what you are going to be thinking tomorrow.

~Glen Beaman

If nothing ever changed, there'd be no butterflies.

~Author Unknown

Nowadays change is around every corner;
in my day it was only around the expected ones.

~V.L. Allineare

We did not change as we grew older; we just became more clearly ourselves.

~Lynn Hall

It is not the strongest of the species that survive, nor the most intelligent,
but the one most responsive to change.

~Author unknown, commonly misattributed to Charles Darwin

The wheel of change moves on, and those who were down go up and those who were up go down.

~Jawaharlal Nehru

Those who expect moments of change to be comfortable and free of conflict have not learned their history.

~Joan Wallach Scott

After you've done a thing the same way for two years, look it over carefully.
After five years, look at it with suspicion. And after ten years, throw it away and start all over.

~Alfred Edward Perlman, *New York Times*, 3 July 1958

Continuity gives us roots; change gives us branches, letting us stretch and grow and reach new heights.

~Pauline R. Kezer

If you would attain to what you are not yet, you must always be displeased by what you are. For where you are pleased with yourself there you have remained.
Keep adding, keep walking, keep advancing.

~Saint Augustine

Every beginning is a consequence - every beginning ends something.

~Paul Valery

It's the most unhappy people who most fear change.

~Mignon McLaughlin, *The Second Neurotic's Notebook*, 1966

God grant me the serenity to accept the people I cannot change, the courage to change the one I can, and the wisdom to know it's me.

~Author Unknown

We all have big changes in our lives that are more or less a second chance.

~Harrison Ford

If you want to truly understand something, try to change it.

~Kurt Lewin

Things do not change; we change.

~Henry David Thoreau

Our only security is our ability to change.

~John Lilly

Because things are the way they are, things will not stay the way they are.

~Bertold Brecht

Things alter for the worse spontaneously, if they be not altered for the better designedly.

~Francis Bacon

A scholar who loves comfort is not fit to be called a scholar.

~Confucius, *Analects*

Every possession and every happiness is but lent by chance for an uncertain time, and may therefore be demanded back the next hour.

~Arthur Schopenhauer

DO YOU HAVE ANY CONSCIOUS OR UNCONSCIOUS LIMITING DECISION IN REGARDS TO WHAT YOU WANT?

You have the power within to succeed or fail at just about anything. The greatest limitations we have are in our beliefs. If you believe that you can succeed at something, chances are you will. If you do not believe that you will succeed, then success will only be an accident. Our beliefs are the programming by which our unconscious minds lead our lives.

Limiting beliefs reduce our options; empowering beliefs increase them; so it is important not only to stay positive about the results of your journey toward your goal, you must actually have the empowering belief that you will succeed. If you have a limiting belief about your ability to achieve, you will sabotage your efforts.

NLP offers a number of different techniques that can help you identify and remove your limiting beliefs and remove any conscious or unconscious limiting decisions.

One way that has been around for a long time to help program your mind is positive affirmations. If you've spent any time at all in the self-development arena, you know that these are short phrases that program the unconscious mind towards a goal in a positive and succinct fashion.

The phrases that are used are short and to the point. They do not leave any room for doubt. Many times these phrases begin with "I AM". This puts the changes in the present tense. Here is an example:

"I am healthy and at the peak of fitness today and every day."

This simple phrase, when repeated, gives the unconscious mind an image. When you are saying this affirmation you are imagining what you look and feel like at the peak of fitness. The unconscious mind is given this snapshot, and then directs your behaviors toward this goal in order to create this image. Here is an example of an affirmation that IS NOT structured correctly.

"I want to lose some weight."

This indicates that you "want" something but leaves it open for doubt. In addition there is no timeframe. Remember that the unconscious mind works on the principle of least resistance, and will not work more than it has to, so you need to give it a timeframe. You are also asking for it to lose something rather than gain something. This puts the mind in a negative frame, as it implies you have something bad or have done something bad to be overweight.

Here is another example of a well-written affirmation:

"I am a loving person and I attract other loving people to me."

Again, the "I AM" establishes a timeframe—NOW. You are stating in a positive way that you are a loving person and because you are a loving person it is only natural that other loving people will be attracted to you.

Here is another one:

"I am prosperous and today I will bring even more abundance into my life."

This one establishes you are not only successful right now, but that you will attract even more abundance into your life.

Once you establish your goals, affirmations are an easy yet powerful tool to use not only to program your mind for what you want, but to also program your mind for success through positive thinking.

I have recently found a more powerful way to do affirmations. This comes from Noah St. John and Denise Bérard's book entitled *The Great Little Book of Afformations*, where they explain that there is a better way to direct your mind toward what you want, which they call *Afformations*.

You see, *affirmation* comes from the Latin word *firmare*, to make firm; *afformation*, on the other hand, comes from the Latin word *formare*, to form or to give shape. But there is another principle of the mind at work in Afformations.

Let me ask you a few questions, and notice what happens inside your mind as you contemplate them.

What did you have for breakfast yesterday?

What was the color of the room you grew up in?

What is your favorite movie?

Did you notice what happened after you finished reading each question? That's right. Your mind started searching for an answer. We are hardwired to look for answers to questions, and that is the basic premise of why afformations work so much better.

You may say "I am a loving person and attract other loving people to me" and you may believe it, but there is a chance you may reject it, isn't there?

But notice what happens when you ask yourself, "How am I a loving person, and how is it that I attract other loving people to me?" Do you notice the difference?

If you're like most people, your mind started searching for the proof to fulfill that question.

That's also how sometimes we mess ourselves up with the disempowering questions we ask ourselves, "Why doesn't anybody love me?" "How come I'm so unlucky" "Why do bad things always happen to me?"

Direct your mind toward what you want, not toward what you don't want. Remember that you get what you focus on, so focus on what you want.

PARTS INTEGRATION

Remember earlier in the book you learned that NLP works better with the whole mind rather than in parts. Sometimes we can become fragmented in our lives and it is important to do a parts integration, which brings these parts back into alignment with one another.

If you've ever thought or said to yourself, "Part of me wants this, but part of me doesn't" or "Sometimes I feel like I'm never enough" you're probably dealing with a parts conflict.

This fragmentation can be the result of our different roles being at odds with one another. These roles can mean that we have different goals, perceptions and beliefs. Part of the process of parts integration is to seek out these internal conflicts and be able to identify them. An NLP Practitioner can help you through this process. Once you have identified these conflicts you will need to negotiate or work with each of these parts both separately and together. Through this work, the parts will begin to align with one another again and you will remove the conflicts.

In our live NLP Practitioner and NLP Master Practitioner trainings we delve deeply into this effective and straightforward process, so be sure to attend the next one.

One of the most efficient ways of creating your life as your masterpiece is seizing every opportunity to be happy... being in the moment. You don't need a long dull life, but rather a happiness-filled life. So even if you're in the twilight of your life, seize the day NOW.

"The butterfly counts not days but moments and has time enough."

(Rabindranath Tagore, poet, philosopher, author, songwriter, painter,

educator, composer, Nobel laureate; 1861-1941)

ᎠAIN VS. PLEASURE

✦ ✦ ✦

EARLIER WE MENTIONED THE PRINCIPLE OF Pain vs. Pleasure when we talked about Propulsion Systems, and the Toward and Away From motivators. Let's delve deeper into this powerful catalyst for change.

One of the ways your mind works where motivation is concerned is the constant struggle between the forces of pain and pleasure. Many behaviors are managed by either your aversion to pain or your attachment to pleasure. Consider your desk at work. If it is a wreck it can be because of a couple of different reasons. The first scenario is that there is more pain associated with organizing your desk than pleasure, and therefore you don't tackle it. The other scenario is that it is not painful enough to clean it and you like having it a wreck.

Tony Robbins, a world-renowned motivational speaker and writer, has a system of change that is based upon making life feel bad enough to change it, or making your goal feel sweet enough to keep pursuing it. Many people struggle with things like weight or even relationships, because of this ongoing internal struggle.

This is very true of people who are trying to fight an addiction. There are many great programs available that can help people deal with their addictions, but their success rates do not seem to be very good. This is because if people are forced into these types of programs or are not ready to quit, it does not matter what type of program they try, it will not succeed.

The reason they do not work is because the pleasure of the addiction is much greater than the desire to stop. They are not in enough "pain" yet. This is because they have not hit bottom. The high that they get from the addiction is greater than any pain they are experiencing in their lives right now.

Once they have hit rock bottom, this is the time that change can occur. This is true of many behaviors. There is an exercise that demonstrates how to overcome unwanted behaviors in order to achieve your life goals and begin to paint the masterpiece that is your life.

The exercise is called the "Dickens Pattern," and is based on Charles Dickens' story *A Christmas Carol.* In the tale, the main character is visited by three spirits, because of his negative behaviors. After being shown his past, present and future, the pain of his deeds overcame his pleasure at being a greedy miser.

The Dickens Pattern exercise follows this same story line. It looks at the past, present and future of a particular behavior or situation. Consider the scenario of being overweight by more than 40 pounds. You look at your past and see how much the extra weight has sabotaged your health, relationships, and happiness. This may make you feel the pain from the past, and you might feel awful about it.

Next you can look at your situation in the present. You may feel that everything is rotten in your life because you're overweight. Then you look at the future, maybe 5 years later, 10 years later, or even 50 years later —if you've even made it that far—, and see how miserable your life is because you're still overweight. The pain will overcome any pleasure you might have in staying overweight. When you finally open your eyes, you're suddenly all guns blazing as you throw the ice cream out of your house and lock yourself in the gym.

Consider some of the behaviors you are stuck with. Are they motivated by pain or pleasure? Remember that pain and pleasure are two sides of the same coin. They are registered in the same part of the brain. So these types of habits need a little extra help to overcome. NLP can help turn this coin in order to facilitate change.

Part of the process is looking at what is the root of the issue. In the example above concerning weight, the root could be comfort. Perhaps when you were growing up, food meant home, comfort and protection, so eating brings you these pleasurable feelings. So, the real issue is not eating; it is whatever is making you need the feeling of comfort and security. You can then decide if there is something you need to remove from your life—like a bad relationship—or whether there is something lacking, such as job satisfaction.

NLP can help the mind release the pleasure it receives from bad habits. It does not replace it with pain; it merely opens up the possibilities for more acceptable behaviors that assist us in creating our life as a masterpiece.

YOU HAVE STRATEGIES

✦ ✦ ✦

WE ALL HAVE STRATEGIES. These are the programs we are running inside ourselves. They are like computer programs that have icons on your screen. Every time you double-click them, the same program comes up. These are similar to the strategies we have. Whenever a certain situation comes up, it activates a certain strategy within us. We have many different programs/strategies that we use every day.

If you can learn a person's strategy for dealing with certain situations, it can be advantageous. For instance, suppose you are a salesman. If you know a particular customer's buying strategy, you can know better how to sell a particular product to them. Knowing their buying strategy means that you know their needs and what their thought process is in buying.

Another way this is advantageous to you is if you are a parent. If you know your child's different strategies for, say, trying something new, you'll know the best way to get them to eat healthy foods or new foods. We are creatures of habit, and strategies are evidence of this fact. We will repeat the same program every time we receive the same stimulus. So it is important as a parent to teach children the right strategies so that they are making the right decisions. We can run useful strategies or unresourceful strategies.

The problem that a lot of people have with strategies is that they allow the strategies to run them, rather than learning to run their own strategies. They live on the Effect side of life, and allow the strategies to run over and over again, without much hope or movement to stop the strategies, and program new ones. NLP is great at creating these new strategies.

Consider the strategy of reassurance. This is the ability to make yourself feel good about the decisions that you make. If you could have control over this program, you would know how to reassure yourself about your decisions. It would build confidence and courage. Being able to understand and even creating the strategy can be yet another brush stroke in the masterpiece of the life you are creating.

Look at some of the strategies you use every day. In the United States, whenever April 15 rolls around people get nervous. It is because they are not really motivated to do their taxes, so as tax time approaches they try to put it off as long as possible. Imagine what it would be like if you could reprogram your motivation strategy. Instead of the pain of worry and procrastination, you will be able to whiz right through that task with joy.

Consider for a moment the definition of a strategy. Human experience is an endless sequence series of representations—it is nothing more than a chain of internal representations. These are like mini-movies of sight and sound. Some other sensory data can be a part of it, too, such as the internal dialogue that takes place, but sight and sound are the main components of these chains. A strategy is a specific chain. We run the same exact chain in the same situations. Regardless of the size of the decision we are making, we run through the same program.

In the case of a customer and their buying strategy, the same strategy is run whether they are buying a loaf of bread or buying a new car. They run through the same program with certain strategies and components. This is why some good salespeople will get to know their customer and ask questions to get a sense of the strategy the customer uses. Do they look for it being made in the USA? Do they look for consumer reports? Do they look for quality over price? All of these types of strategies are important to consider.

When you are creating the masterpiece that is your life, consider the strategies you use in your decision-making. Do they work for you? Do they hinder you? Consider how these strategies were formed. How long have you been using them? Have they been useful or do they need to be rewritten. NLP is a great way to write new strategies while retiring old ones.

$\mathcal{L}$OVE STRATEGY

✦ ✦ ✦

IN NLP THERE IS THE CONCEPT OF ANCHORS, which comes from Behavioral Psychology. Anchors are thoughts or patterns of thought that keep you attached to an idea or place in your life. Like strategies, anchors can be good or they can be harmful.

The process of anchoring in NLP is when you associate memory recall, state change or other responses with some stimulus, in such a way that perception of the stimulus (the anchor) leads by reflex to the anchored response occurring. Many times this stimulus is neutral and at times out of conscious awareness. The response to the anchor may be either positive or negative. These anchors are formed and reinforced by repetition.

This is similar to the process of classical conditioning in which the pairing of two unrelated stimuli is formed. The most famous version was when a scientist, Ivan Pavlov, paired the sound of a tuning fork and food, within a dog. The dog would salivate when the food was presented. A tuning fork was rung whenever the food was presented. This was repeated over and over again. After a time, just the sound of the tuning fork without the food made the dog salivate. Anchors are formed in our minds much the same way. Repetition, timing and intensity are the keys to effective and lasting anchors.

One of the things that NLP can do is create these anchors with a client by associating one response to another, or between an external stimulus and an internal response in one trial.

The basic form of anchoring in NLP is creating a strong, congruent experience of a desired state; while at the same time using some distinct stimulus (touch, word, and image) at the time the experience is at its peak. When done correctly, repetition of the stimulus will re-associate and restore the experience of the state.

TYPES OF ANCHORS

There are many different types of anchors with different triggers, such as verbal phrases, physical touches or sensations, certain sights and sounds, or internally, such as the words we say to ourselves, or memories and emotional states.

For all intents and purposes, everything you perceive acts as an anchor, in the sense that perceiving it tends to bring up some thought, feeling or response.

As mentioned earlier, the natural process of creating an anchor can be good or bad. For example, a voice tonality that resembles the characteristics of one's perception of an "angry voice" may not actually be as a result of anger, but will usually trigger an emotional response in the person perceiving the tonality to have the traits of anger.

There are certain sets of circumstances that usually need to occur in order for an anchor to be formed.

Most NLP Trainers agree that the trigger must be:

Specific - otherwise the subject will not begin to react to it

Intermittent or Timed Right - if it were constant, then you would no longer be sensitive to it.

Anchored to a unique, specific and prompt reaction - otherwise the anchor would not elicit a response to it, because there would be too many different reactions being associated to the trigger.

It is also important that reinforcement of an anchor (in other words, repeated formation with the aim of reinforcement) should have a time of rest between the times it is repeated.

HERE ARE SOME EXAMPLES OF ANCHORS AND HOW THEY EXIST IN OUR LIVES:

When you were a child you may have participated in family activities that gave you great pleasure, the pleasure was associated with the activity itself, so when you think of the activity or are reminded of it you tend to re-experience some pleasurable feeling.

If you are looking through a family photo album, there may be a stir of pleasant memories and some of the feelings associated with them.

A child's comforter can help comfort them in an unfamiliar situation, because of the anchor the comforter represents—safety.

Sometimes an old love song can re-awaken a romantic mood.

The smell of freshly baked apple pies brings back memories of visits to your grandmother's house and the fond memories of those times.

Phobias in this sense can be studied as one example of a very powerful anchor—see spider; feel terrified and nauseous.

Revisiting an old school or a place with powerful memories.

In relationships, we can form negative anchors. These can trigger feelings and coping strategies that can hurt a relationship. It is important to realize this, as these anchors sometimes need to be released and new anchors formed in order for us to develop more meaningful and healthy relationships.

An example of how a negative anchor can form in a relationship is comforting someone when they are upset. We might give a person a hug whenever we see that they are in emotional distress. Over time, this simple act can create an anchor associated with the hug. Whenever the person gives you a hug you may immediately have a response of emotional turmoil. This is not intentional, but it can have a negative impact upon a relationship. The issue is that this comforting gesture can collapse the negative emotion at first. But it begins to build, and the hug then becomes associated with those negative emotions.

An NLP Practitioner working with couples knows how to elicit deep love strategies. These are the strategies we use when we are truly in love with someone. It is important to remember that whomever the person is looking at when the deep love strategy is evoked can become the object of that affection. This is why NLP Practitioners will often have a person facing away from them when they activate it, or they will have the person face their partner. These types of deep love strategies are very powerful and can be used as the basis to rebuild broken relationships, and should only be used under the care of a trained NLP professional.

There are other anchors, both positive and negative, that can be formed in relationships. These can make a relationship feel stuck, and couples may notice they are having the same types of arguments over and over again. This is because their strategies have become intertwined, and one phrase will set off a person's relationship strategy and then their response may trigger the other person's defense strategy. This can go on for months or years, unless a new script is formed and breaks the cycle.

So, HOW ARE YOU DOING? – READY, FIRE, AIM

✦ ✦ ✦

AS WE NEAR THE END OF THIS BOOK, you have learned many different aspects of NLP and what it can do for you. You have become acquainted with your mind—your canvass—and the different techniques and processes you can use to Create Your Life as Your Masterpiece. And sometimes on our journey in life we need help from guides and tutors. NLP workers are those guides and tutors.

As you move through your journey with your outcomes in mind, you will revise and adjust your actions constantly. A plane is off-course most of the time. A pilot will make adjustments. A flight is never in a straight line. They must reevaluate where they are, and make necessary adjustments. Sometimes they will call into a tower to help them see where they are and whether they are off-course. Your tower operator is a trained NLP Practitioner. They can help you see where you are and how to adjust your direction to get back on your path.

Management guru Tom Peters popularized the "Ready, Fire, Aim" strategy, as opposed to the traditional "Ready, Aim, Fire" of marksmanship, which causes people to suffer from Analysis-Paralysis, or being so afraid of making a wrong turn that they NEVER move.

Many people have an internal fear of failure, so they stop trying. If they do not try then they can never fail. The reality is that failure becomes your best friend. Not trying becomes automatic failure.

Successful people fail a great deal because they make a lot of attempts. It is through this process of failure that we learn and grow. When you are paralyzed, like a statue, you will be unable to go anywhere in life.

The great baseball player Babe Ruth held the homerun record and the strikeout record at the same time. This meant he has just as many failures as successes, but he would not have any successes, unless he tried.

Those who have the most successes also have the most failures. There is nothing wrong or shameful in failing. Most people do not look back and regret their failures, they regret the things that they never tried or pursued.

You can either use NLP techniques and have some successes and failures or not even try NLP and never know how it may have transformed your life. The great thing about NLP is that you can make adjustments along the way. It's the ready-fire-aim approach and, surprisingly, it works a lot better than the more common ready-aim-fire approach.

Once you take a chance and fire, you can refine your next shot and make the adjustments in your aim. You could get bogged down with preparation and never fire. That's why firing first can give you important information and keep you moving. How many potentially great ideas have you passed up because you got stuck in the state of analysis paralysis (i.e. ready-aim-aim-aim-aim-aim...)?

The opposite of success is not failure; the opposite of success is stagnation—inaction. In fact failure is part of success. In order to achieve anything worthwhile in your life, you have to take a chance, fail, learn from it, and try again. The great thing about success is that no one will remember your failures, anyway. Actor Jim Carey was booed off many a stage while a young comedian. We have electric light bulbs because Thomas Edison refused to give up even after thousands of failed experiments. Reframe the word "failure": You either succeed, or you have a learning experience. *There is no failure, only feedback.*

Fear will freeze you in place. You have to let it go. Remember that baggage we talked about. Part of that baggage is fear of failing.

Even if you think you might fail at something, just dive in and see what happens. Don't let fear keep you from the path of success. Success usually does not happen by accident. It takes work and, more importantly, courage.

If you look at people who are successful in business today, you will commonly see that many of them had a string of dismal failures before finally hitting on something that worked, myself included. And I think most of these people will agree that those early failure experiences were an essential contributing factor in their future successes.

Continue with your goal in mind. "Consider the postage stamp: its usefulness consists on sticking to one thing until it gets there." Josh Billings

Remember that with every thought and with every action you are sculpting the Masterpiece of your Life. With every decision and in every situation in your life, make sure you're At Cause.

Do the exercises to find out exactly where you are in your life, and now that you know how your mind works, decide who you want to be and create SMART goals for every area of your life.

Remember that happiness starts from within, and its essential component is balance. Clear the negativity from your past.

Start on some of those incomplete things you listed a while back. This will make more energy available for the other things you wish to accomplish in your life.

Embrace change as the inevitable catalyst for success. Recognize and utilize your strategies to propel you toward your goals, and create new strategies for success.

Keep moving in the direction of your dreams and follow the "Ready-Fire-Aim" strategy, making adjustments until you reach your goals in life.

I hope you have enjoyed this primer on creating the life of your dreams, because Your Life Is Your Masterpiece.

I invite you to check out our training schedule, and consider investing in yourself and in your future.

Check out our website for the current discounts and specials just for readers of *Your Life Is Your Masterpiece*.

And, if you feel that you need help with anything along the way, give us a call at (888) 854-5467 so together we can design the life of your dreams.

Carpe Diem!

www.YourLifeIsYourMasterpiecce.com
[Spanish version: www.TuVidaEsTuObraMaestra.com]

and

there are no unresouceful people - only unresourceful states.

ABOUT THE AUTHOR

✦ ✦ ✦

CÉSAR VARGAS IS A DOCTOR OF CLINICAL HYPNOTHERAPY, Coach, Master Hypnotist, Master Practitioner of Neuro-Linguistic Programming (NLP), Master Practitioner of TIME Techniques. He is the author of the translation of this book *Tu Vida Es Tu Obra Maestra – Consejos prácticos para diseñar tu vida, a propósito* (TuVidaEsTuObraMaestra.com), co-author of the book *Descubre TU Grandeza* and co-author of *Unstuck: The Owners' Manual for Success*, among many others.

He is the translator of *Spiritual Marketing*, by Joe Vitale, *Feelings Buried Alive, Never Die*, by Karol Truman, *Success Secrets of the Rich and Happy*, by Bart Baggett, *The Science of Success* and *Practical Spirituality*, by James Arthur Ray, and *The Science of Getting Rich*, by Wallace D. Wattles, the 1910 classic that was the inspiration for the movie and the book *The Secret*.

Dr. César Vargas offers certifications in Hypnosis and NLP, as well as courses, seminars and workshops on different aspects of personal development.

He has an office in southern California, where he helps clients who come from around the corner and around the globe to get the results they desire.

For more information about Cesar Vargas, log on to DoctorCesar.com or YourLifeIsYourMasterpiece.com.

OTHER RESOURCES FOR YOUR SUCCESS

✦ ✦ ✦

In order to continue the exploration of this marvelous topic—Your Mind—be sure to attend the Live Weekend Course based on this book, *Design Your Life As Your Masterpiece*. Come delve deeply into the topics introduced in this book, and share with others your success. Check out www.YourLifeIsYourMasterpiece.com for the upcoming dates, locations, and ways you can get involved in changing people's lives in your community and around the world.

While you're there check out the additional free resources that you can use to continue Designing Your Life as Your Masterpiece.

Remember, each and every day you're creating something. Whether you're creating a formless mass of abstract art or a true masterpiece you'll be proud to share, depends on the action you take right now!

Special discount for Readers of
Your Life Is Your Masterpiece

Save $200 off the regular price of our weekend seminars:

- **Design Your Life As Your Masterpiece... LIVE!**
- **Intro to NLP**
- **Powerful Presentations**
- **Weekend Hypnosis Course**
- **Certain Goals Workshop**

Simply call 888-854-5467, Ext. 8 and mention savings code: YLIYM

Visit www.YourLifeIsYourMasterpiece.com for further details.

As an unadvertised bonus, and as a thank you for finishing reading the book, and because winners always contribute to the success of others, I'm offering you, my reader, a COMPLIMENTARY 15-MINUTE PHONE CONSULTATION on any issue that you believe I can help you with through any of the techniques mentioned in this book. All you pay is the toll fees, if any. If you're in the Continental United States, I'll even pay for the call. To redeem your Complimentary 15-Minute Phone Consultation, please call 888-854-5467, Extension 8, and mention code: FREE-CONSULT. If you're outside the U.S., email Cesar.Vargas@YourLifeIsYourMasterpiece.com to coordinate how to receive your Complimentary Consultation.

ORDER FORM ON THE OTHER SIDE

VIP

VERITAS INVICTUS PUBLISHING

ORDER FORM

I would like to obtain additional copies of *Your Life Is Your Masterpiece* for me and/or for my family and friends, who are about to make their life A Masterpiece through these powerful mind and action principles.

Name: _____

Address: _____

City: _____ State: _____

Country: _____ Zip Code: _____

Email (for confirmation purposes): _____

Comments (additional on reverse): _____

Amount _____ X $19.95 (USD)   Subtotal $_____

Shipping & Handling   USA & Canada $ 7.50

To Latin America $ 12.50

Email: info@YourLifeIsYourMasterpiece.com   Rest of the world   Please Ask

Total enclosed (USD) $_____

Send this form with your remittance to:

VERITAS INVICTUS PUBLISHING
8502 East Chapman Avenue # 302
Orange, California 92869
United States

$19.95
ISBN 978-1-939180-01-8
51995

9 781939 180018

To obtain your copy via Internet with a credit card, log on to:
www.**Your**L*ife***Is***Your***Masterpiece**.com

www.ingramcontent.com/pod-product-compliance
Lightning Source LLC
Chambersburg PA
CBHW070800100426
42742CB00012B/2206